F DARLINGTON SANDS

120

ENCHANTED SUMMERS

An Illustrated & Social History
of Bowmanville Beach 1900-2020

RICK MCEACHERN & GARY COLE

Tellwell Talent
www.tellwell.ca

ISBN
978-0-2288-3623-0 (Paperback)
978-0-2288-3624-7 (eBook)

Table of Contents

PART TWO

Preface

Some years ago my very good friend Chuck MacDonald said to me "someone should write down the history of this beach before we old-timers cash in our chips and it's all forgotten." That resulted in my first small booklet (A Few Acres of Sand) about the cottages on Harbour Beach. In that booklet, I hinted that someday I would write another book containing the whole history of the West Beach Bowmanville. That idea, due to my lack of ambition and my ingrown laziness stayed on the back burner for a very long time.

But about two years ago, I had the very good fortune of meeting Rick McEachern. This book is the result of Rick's help and interest and it is a plain and simple fact that without him this book would never have seen the light of day nor felt the printer's ink.

All the information contained here is from my reminiscences and the memories of conversations with many people over the years, especially my old friend and mentor Forest Dilling. Although most of the dates amount to guesswork, they are all as accurate as human memory allows. The information is to the best of my memory accurate, and any errors or omissions are purely unintended and are the result of the passing of time and the failing of that memory.

Gary Cole

Preface

Several years ago I read Gary Cole's interesting book, "A Few Acres of Sand". In that booklet, Gary stated that it was not a history of Bowmanville West Beach rather a description of the original cottages and that the history would come later. His booklet perked my curiosity and in the spring of 2018 I set out to find West Beach a place where I had never been. After finding the beach I soon afterwards found Gary Cole at his cottage Rathkeale. During our first conversation, I reminded Gary of his previous promise to write a history of the beach and asked him why he had never done it. He said he simply had never got around to it. I asked him if I helped him would he consider fulfilling that promise and he said he would.

During my time researching and writing this book with Gary I have gained a deep affection for West Beach and the people who live here. I believe it would've been a perfect place for a child to grow up during the 1940s 50s and 60s. The people, the cottages, the water and the sand would have produced wonderful childhood memories.

Gary told me once that he took his first steps at 9 months of age on the front porch of his parent's cottage on West Beach and Gary has spent every year from the 24th of May until Labour Day at the beach for the past 80+ years. He told me once, "I may not have been born on the West Beach Rick but I'm pretty sure I was conceived there".

Gary and I have got to be close friends over the last two years. It's the places we visit and the people we meet during our lives that give our lives meaning and I'm glad that I was able to help put Gary's remembrances down on paper for future generations to enjoy and wonder what it must have been like to grow up in such a magical place.

Rick McEachern

Dedication Gary Cole

I would like to dedicate this book to all the various people I have known on Bowmanville West Beach over all these years. I especially dedicate it to my mother Edith Alice Severs Cole who loved the Beach more than anyone I ever knew.

Dedication Rick McEachern

I would like to dedicate this book to my daughter Jessica Scott- McEachern, without her encouragement and belief in me the publication of this book would not have been possible.

Acknowledgements

We wish to recognize and thank the following people who helped in making this book a reality. They kindly donated their photographs, information, time and enthusiasm. If we have missed anyone, we apologize as all contributions to this book have been valuable.

- John Colville
- Alexandera Deauters
- Nigel Klemencic- Puglisevich
- Mike Lootsma
- Gail MacDonald
- Ron McLean
- Carol Millen
- Bonnie Piper
- Susan Plumpton
- Zetta Rider
- Sidney Rider
- Brent Hooey - Editor

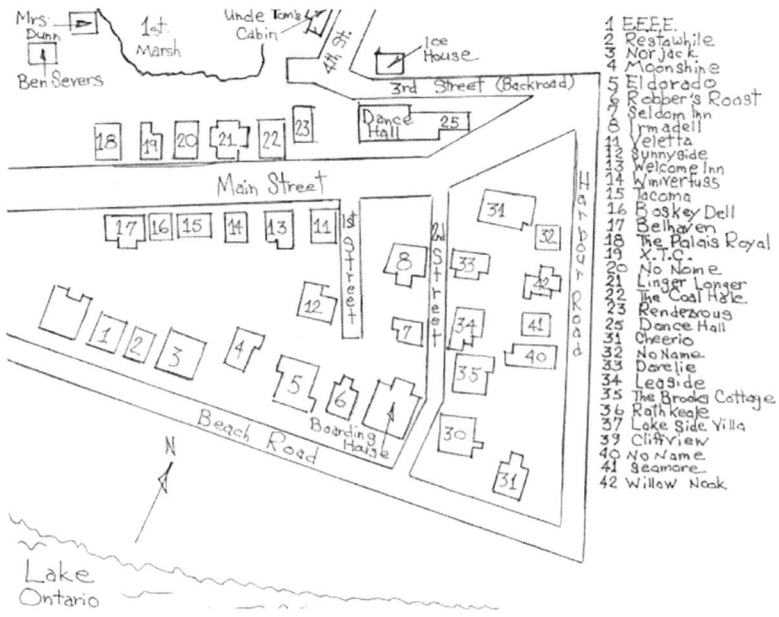

1 E.E.E.E.
2 Restawhile
3 Nor Jack
4 Moonshine
5 Eldorado
6 Robber's Roost
7 Seldom Inn
8 Irmadell
11 Veletta
12 Sunnyside
13 Welcome Inn
14 Winivertuss
15 Tacoma
16 Boskey Dell
17 Belhaven
18 The Palais Royal
19 X.T.C.
20 No Name
21 Linger Longer
22 The Coal Hole
23 Rendezvous
25 Dance Hall
31 Cheerio
32 No Name
33 Darelie
34 Leaside
35 The Brooks Cottage
36 Rath Keale
37 Lake Side Villa
39 Cliffview
40 No Name
41 Seamore
42 Willow Nook

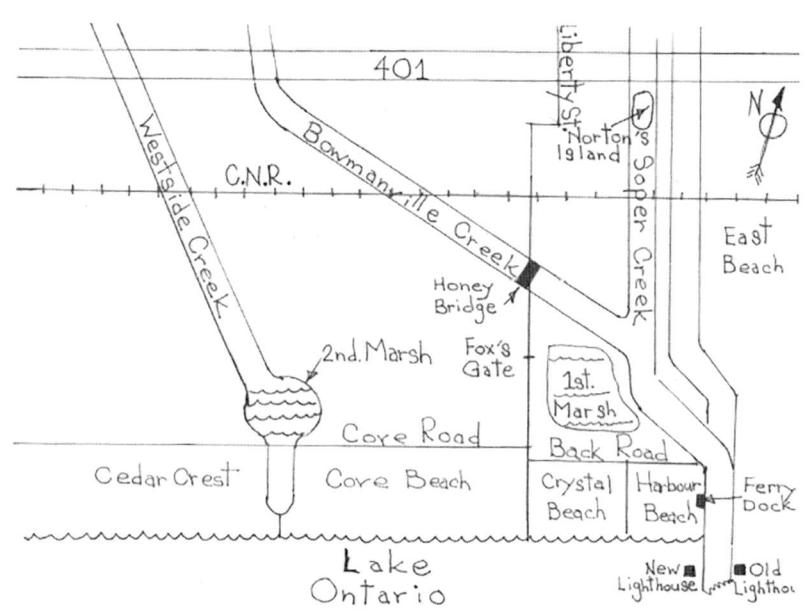

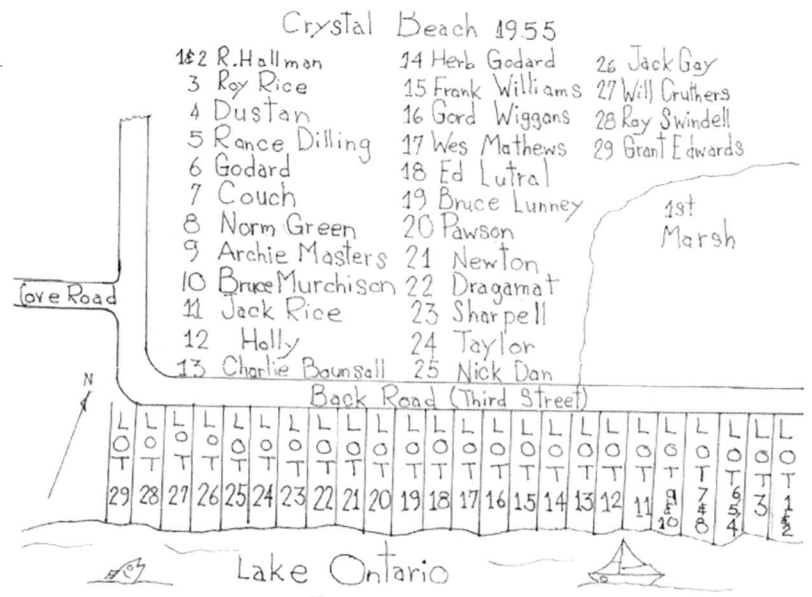

Crystal Beach 1955

1&2 R. Hallman	14 Herb Godard	26 Jack Gay
3 Roy Rice	15 Frank Williams	27 Will Cruthers
4 Dustan	16 Gord Wiggans	28 Ray Swindell
5 Rance Dilling	17 Wes Mathews	29 Grant Edwards
6 Godard	18 Ed Lutral	
7 Couch	19 Bruce Lunney	1st Marsh
8 Norm Green	20 Pawson	
9 Archie Masters	21 Newton	
10 Bruce Murchison	22 Dragamat	
11 Jack Rice	23 Sharpell	
12 Holly	24 Taylor	
13 Charlie Bounsall	25 Nick Dan	

Love Road

Back Road (Third Street)

Lake Ontario

PART ONE

PART TWO

Introduction

Perhaps no similar small vacation area in this province or perhaps the world has the unique character of the Port Darlington Harbour Company lands and the Bowmanville West Beach, in particular.

West Beach was like growing up in a small Ontario village, and the cottages there were the backbone of this village. For over one hundred and twenty years it has been a place where everybody knew, loved and cared for each other. It was truly a place like no other, a real people place.

The development of, Port Darlington as a summer resort received its start during the last decade of the nineteenth century. At that time the more affluent local citizens of Bowmanville built their expensive cottages on East Beach. As a report a few years ago in the Canadian Statesman newspaper said, "On the West Beach, the common folk pitched their tents and built their shacks."

It may be difficult for us to realize today but West Beach was very difficult for people to access one hundred and twenty years ago. There was no legal way to cross the Grand Trunk railway tracks and no road south of the Honey Bridge. The only way to access the West Beach was by boat across the Harbour or by foot. In the early history of the beach, two brothers of the Tait family were of instrumental importance. One brother was named Henry Clay Tait, he was a famous local photographer, who took many photographs of beach activities (some of which are featured elsewhere in this book). The area he photographed became known as Camp Chatter which was located near the Hutchinson cottage (AKA Cliffview/The Hutch). The other brother was the owner of a store on the East Beach, who was also the mayor of Bowmanville at one time. His name was Archie Tait, and he lived in the Octagon House in town. He also owned a grocery store which was where the Coronation Restaurant used to be near the south/west corner of King Street West and Temperance Street. Later people began to build small shacks, these included two legendary groups of young men who called themselves; "The Hungry Six" and "The Cylent Phore". Later the shacks were replaced by small cabins and these were enlarged over the years. This gave rise to a common design on West Beach which consisted of a centre section with a gable roof and later to a lean-to or shed like roof style addition to the front and back as families grew and finances permitted. Roughly two-thirds of the beach cottages were of this basic design with various modifications. As is often the case the situation recorded in the Statesman was not completely accurate.

The first cottage built on the West Beach was a first-class structure that rivalled any of the "swanky" cottages on the East Beach and was owned for many years by one of Bowmanville's most prominent and wealthy citizens. The majority of cottages were built before the First World War and after a wartime lull; most of the rest were constructed. The Cottages that have four-sided hipped roofs were built in the 1930s. For example the Hutchinson's Cliffview, Matthew's Tacoma, and Ben Sever's Lazy Dazy which was the last to be built in 1948.

The oldest cottage was Professor Chester New's Lakeside Villa. Other older Cottages included the western part of the Dancehall, the centre section of Cheerio, the Hughes cottage Leaside, and the Varco's Restawhile. All but three cottages had names during their existence and some had more than one name, adding colour and some class to the beach.

West Beach was the place where almost anyone could afford to own a cottage and over the years the residents formed a wide spectrum of very colourful characters. Among them were almost all parts of the early 20th century Ontario society. Ranging from the fairly well-off to those not so financially fortunate. They ranged from Professor Dr. Chester W. New to Toronto Maple Leaf hockey great Sid Smith and Lord Roy Thompson to Hi Raby. But on the beach somehow everyone fit-in and seemed to be on an equal footing.

As I have said the beach was like a small village and like all villages it had all the services required to lead a simple life. Over the years it boasted: a local police force, a fire brigade, sanitation services, mail delivery, icemen, peddlers, a hotel, a church, a general store, and a community centre. It provided entertainment, sporting activities and all-around fun or its residents and many visitors.

The "land situation" resulted in insecurity of tenancy among the beach residence. For all of their existence, the Harbor Beach (and Crystal Beach until the 1930s which was also leased land) cottages were built on land which was leased from the Port Darlington Harbour Company. Unfortunately over the years, this led to the growth of a feeling of insecurity. It seems that every year some form of problem would arise and there was always the fear of the eviction by the Harbour Company. During WWII it was rumoured and strongly believed that an airbase was being planned. Many people believed that the Saint Lawrence Seaway would flood the beach area. The ongoing problem with the railway crossing, Mrs. W. Fox's gate and the major flood of 1947 all helped to increase this insecurity. This led many of the residents to be very leery about spending too much money on improving their properties. This was compounded by the fact that most were in the lower-income bracket and didn't have much money to spend anyway. This led (especially after the 1950s) to a mindset of, "don't fix it just patch-it." Over the ensuing years, many people for various reasons lost interest in their cottages and simply moved away. As a result of this mindset, by the year 2000, only seven cottages were still occupied, and the remaining twenty-six cottages were abandoned and dilapidated. In 2008 the Municipality of Clarington expropriated the Harbour Company's lands on West Beach and leased them back to the seven remaining residents and some feeling of security was achieved.

Although at first the expropriation was viewed as one step closer to the end of the Harbor Beach as a cottage community. But after a short period of apprehension, the seven remaining residents realized that the expropriation and resulting new park was the best thing that could have happened to them. The park is enjoyed by hundreds of yearly visitors who mix with the residents and share their love of the beach. The Municipality has installed a five-year lease program for the beach residents and have renewed them twice since. The continuation of our hundred twenty years cottage community seems secure for the foreseeable future. For interest sake, it should be noted that the seven remaining residents were: Judy and Sharon Hutchinson, Shirley

Fowler, Don and Donna Adams, Jean Severs, Ted Bounsal, Gail and Chuck MacDonald, and Gary Cole. All are fifty-year residents and many are lifetime beachers. They would all like to thank the Town of Clarington for their help in maintaining our community and all it has stood for over so many years. We would also like to thank the various members of the Town Council and their staff who we have worked with for the last fifteen years. Of special note are former Regional Councillor Willie Woo and our very special friend Ms. Faye Langmaid both of who have been there for us and we cannot thank them enough.

I have spent seventy-seven years on West Beach and seen it in most of its manifestations, and various changes. Through my memories and those of people who came before me especially Forest Dilling, I can now relate one hundred and twenty years of West Beach history. From Pop Quinn and Joe Dilling right up to the present day, I can truly say I can't think of any place in the world where I would rather have spent my life. My only regret is the fact that so many old friends and fine people have moved away and did not get to enjoy what the West Beach has now become. It feels like things have come full circle, right back to the good old days before the war. Unfortunately, those who left don't know and will never know what they have missed.

The father of one of my best childhood friends once told me: "Gary you'll never amount to anything, forty years from now you'll still be wandering around this beach looking at the seagulls.

Unfortunately for me, he was right in the first part, as I never made much of myself. But fortunately for me, he was also right in the second part. I am still wandering around this beach and I have loved every minute of the last seventy-seven years and yes I do like seagulls.

Description of the Sections
of Bowmanville Beach

Bowmanville Beach consists of several different sections, with the central division being the harbour. Everything located on the east side of the harbour is known as East Beach. While everything situated to the west side of the harbour is generally known as West Beach. Since the main topic of our interest in these stories is West Beach, it has several smaller sections. The proper name for West Beach is what is generally called "The Sandbar"; which runs from the turn in the road down to the harbour and the Sandbar parts are:

The Harbor Beach (Sandbar).
The Crystal Beach (Sandbar).
The Cove (Solid ground).
The Second Marsh.
The Cedar Crest (Sandbar).
The Point (Where The Boys Training School Camp was once located).

Coal Sheds 1930

Cylent Phore Crystal Beach   1903

Port Darlington Harbour History

The first beginnings of Bowmanville Beach occurred when the harbour was built and the lands on the shore of Lake Ontario were developed. This location was south of where the grand trunk railroad would later be built. It should be remembered that West Beach was, in reality, a sandbar fronted by Lake Ontario and backed by the 1st marsh and which was created by the construction of the harbour in 1837. The Port Darlington Harbor Company was chartered by the Colonial Government of Upper Canada (Ontario) in 1837 just before Queen Victoria coming to the throne. The Port Darlington Harbor Company was publicly-traded so anyone could buy shares. One of the primary movers and shakers of the company was John Simpson who was the leading citizen of Bowmanville at that time. He was the first president of the company and in later life, he became a member of the Canadian Senate in 1867 the time of Canada's Confederation.

The men who originally formed the Port Darlington Harbor Company met for that purpose in the Hine's Hotel on the north/east corner of Scugog and King Street in 1837.

Originally the outlet of the river was at the western end of the beach in the location of the Parkette today. The Harbour Company built the wharf and the lighthouse where they are today and they dug a new path for the river, which is what it follows today. In the beginning, the water was going in both directions making Bowmanville West Beach an island. But later as the waves silted up the old outlet, it was closed off. There was a rumour which persisted for many years, that the harbour company's land was, in fact, Crown Land and that the harbour company took out a 99- year lease on it. This rumour has now been proven to be false.

The harbour company bought the land from the farmers who owned it. The name of the farmer who owned the West Beach land was Mr. Frank, and the farmer who owned the East Beach was Mr. Smart. The company bought four or five acres of land on each side of where the river is now. The company didn't build anything on the West Beach, but on the East Beach they built the lighthouse, 2-grain elevators, coal shed, an engine house, an office and weigh scales. The main thing shipped out of Darlington Harbour was grain, and its primary destination was the United States. The main thing that was imported in to Darlington Harbour was coal which was brought up from Pennsylvania via the Erie Canal to Oswego New York. Since in those days there were no roads or railroads, schooners moved the coal and grain. In those days almost every town along the shore of Lake Ontario had a port. Between Bowmanville in the west and Port Hope in the east, there was Port Darlington, Newcastle Harbour, Port Britain, Port Granby, and Port Hope. So in those days the amount of traffic by schooner on the great lake of Ontario was quite extensive. Other items were also imported or exported along with the grain and the coal out of Port Darlington.

SS Argyll, along with a few other passenger steamers, also worked out on Port Darlington. The Port Darlington Harbour Company also erected a lighthouse on the East Pier. That lighthouse building was the size and shape of a house with board and batten siding, and it was painted an off-white colour and it had a tower to hold the light.

There were two Lighthouse keepers; the first was named Tom Norton who lived south of the railroad tracks. There was an island in the river called Norton's Island named after him. The other lighthouse keeper was Tom Orr who lived on the East Beach. Tom Orr tragically died when the lighthouse was struck by lightning while he was inside. The harbourmaster lived in a rather substantial house on the East Beach just north of where the grain elevators were located. Later this building became Christie's boarding house. The first person to occupy the harbourmaster's house was John McClellan, whose real title was wharfinger. After Mr. McClellan's death, his son James McClellan took over. James, who was also the manager of the Bank of Montreal, lived in the town of Bowmanville on Church Street almost across the street from St. Pauls United Church. James was also involved in a lumber and coal company called, McClellan and Cann which was in the location where the Veltri apartment building is today. After James left the harbour company, his son Guernsey McClellan who lived in Toronto, ran it.

Between 1900 and 1910 the harbour business was starting to peter-out because of competition from two railroads that had arrived in town. Over the years the Harbour Company leased out the land on both East and West Beach for cottagers to build their cottages. The lighthouse was a real lighthouse with a rotating and magnifying light which was lit by a kerosene lamp. The lighthouse keeper had to light the kerosene lamp every night during the summer, spring, and fall season. During the 1920s the police who patrolled the lake caught a ship which was running rum and brought her into Bowmanville harbour loaded with quart bottles of beer. The police impounded the ship and put her in the coal sheds for safekeeping. Unfortunately for the police much of the beer was stolen by some thirsty locals. One night shortly after that the coal sheds and the ship caught fire and both were destroyed.

Driving piles down into the soft muck of the harbour river bed made the inland part of the harbour. Once the harbour builders got out into the lake, they could no longer drive piles, so they built what they called cribs. These cribs were built out into the lake and made of massive timbers similar to telephone poles which were all spiked together. The cribs then filled with fieldstone causing them to sink to the bottom of the lake. The cribs that were built from the harbour out into the lake in 1837 are still intact today. Old Great Lake schooners known as stone hookers sailed close into shore where they would pick up loads of large stones. When the ships were full, they would go to the harbour and dump their load of rocks into the cribs.

The harbour business started to peter out around the start of the First World War. The most famous ship ever to sail into Port Darlington Harbor was the Oliver Mowat. Sir Oliver Mowat was the Liberal Premier of Ontario from around 1870 until almost 1900.

The McClellan family who owned the harbour company were very staunch Liberals, and so they named the ship after the Ontario Premier. The Oliver Mowat had two masts as did most great lake schooners. Premier Oliver Mowat was related to the famous author Farley Mowat; he would have been an uncle to Farley Mowat's father.

As the harbour company started to fail around 1918 – 1920, the engine room and the office building were converted into cottages. Since building material was scarce at the end of WWI, the lumber was used to build cottages. Even though the harbour company was on its last legs, the cottagers on the beach still had to pay their lease payments. Gary Cole remembers that his dad had to pay the harbour company $5 per year. In 1948-49, the federal government paid to have dredging ships called sand suckers dredge out the harbour. The sand sucker which worked in Port Darlington was named: "Black Carrier." It was a converted troop carrier like those used on D-Day. There were still fishermen in business in those days even though the harbour company had gone out of business by then.

The men who originally formed the Darlington Harbor Company met in the Hines Hotel on the north/east corner of Scugog and King Street in 1834. Bruce Berry, a longtime resident of the Bowmanville West Beach, says that there was a hotel on the east side of the harbour, where sailors and travellers could stay. Lost in the sands of time are the name of the hotel and its exact location. A downtown Bowmanville livery stable owner named Mr. Glover had an omnibus which he used to carry passengers from ships docked at Darlington Harbour, uptown to the hotel.

Legendary Shipwrecks
of Port Darlington

Around the time of WWI in the vicinity of the Second Marsh, someone got the idea to get gravel from the shore in front of Cedar Crest Beach. There were no cottages there then just vacant land. They used two ships, the Juno, which was a metal freighter and the Erie Bell, which was a wooden schooner. These two ships were sunk in the water off the Second Marsh and used as temporary piers for a harbour. Ships would tie up there and load up with gravel. Around 1923 these ships were abandoned. The wooden schooner, Erie Bell, started to break up. Since the rib cage could still float and with the action of the waves and the wind, it ended up drifting down to Bowmanville Beach. Since it was an eyesore, years later one of the cottagers ended up setting it on fire one night. Much to the chagrin of the beach kids who enjoyed playing on the wreck. When Gary Cole's father Fred was a child of about ten years of age; he would play pirates with his friends on the deck of the schooner. The Juno, on the other hand, is still there under the waves, and every year skin divers come and dive on the wreck.

Around the World War 1 era, there was another metal ship which had seen better days, and it was being towed up to Toronto to be broken up for scrap. When they got off of Port Darlington, she started to sink, so they had to cut the line and let her go. She's out there under the waves of Port Darlington still, and although searched for, for many years she has yet to be found. The fact that her location has remained elusive is not surprising considering that Lake Ontario is the second deepest of the Great Lakes.

Port Darlington Fishermen

At one time Port Darlington supported an active fishing industry. Up until the mid-1950s, three fishing boats working out of Port Darlington Harbour. They fished for Whitefish, Lake Trout, and Cisco (a type of herring). Their ships were about 20 ft long, and the best-known of these was the "Audrey" which was owned by Fred Depew and named after his wife. Fred's brother Charlie Depew also was a fisherman out of Darlington Harbour. While Fred Depew was the best-known fisherman, with one man (Harry March) and one boy working for him; Charlie was the biggest with his two sons (Tom and Harry) and two other men working for him during the fishing season. Charlie's son Tom (who was very popular around town) was an excellent hockey player. He played junior hockey and would undoubtedly have made the NHL had he not developed arthritis which unfortunately cut his hockey career short. One of the people Tom played junior hockey with was Ernie Dickens. Ernie was from Saskatchewan, and in the summer he also came and worked on Charlie's boat. Ernie later played in the NHL for the Boston Bruins and then the Toronto Maple Leafs.

After his NHL career, Ernie settled in Bowmanville and worked in either General Motors or Goodyear.

Another local Bowmanville man, Jack Hatley also fished out of Darlington Harbor. Jack also owned a garage in Bowmanville, and tragically around 1930, there were a fire and explosion in his garage; which killed a mechanic named Mr. Gatchel whose wife looked after the boarding house on Bowmanville Beach.

11Frank Blunt also worked for Jack Hatley, and in the mid-1950s the Canadian government put a bombing range out in front of Bowmanville Beach which unfortunately put an end to the fishing industry here. Planes came up from Trenton Ontario to practice bombing runs. The fishermen were only able to fish three days a week, and the fish stocks were also starting to peter at that time.

The fish that were caught by the fishermen were packed in wooden boxes and covered with ice. Taken to the nearby railway station for shipment they went to places like New York City. Fish from Lake Ontario ended up as meals in some of the biggest NYC restaurants such as the Waldorf Astoria.

As the fish stock started to peter out, Fred Depew was paid by the Canadian government to give up his fishing license and stop fishing. His boat ended up in Brighton, Ontario where another fisherman who was still fishing used it.

There was also another fisherman named Lord Burton who fished out of a rowboat with a small sail. Lord Burton lived in the cottage which was at the end of Crystal Beach (latter owned by Grant Edwards). Two Scottish brothers fished out of East Beach. One brother was called Captain Matheson, and his bagpipe playing brother was named Malcolm. These fishermen used gill nets which were set one day and pulled up the next. Generally, two men would work together, with one pulling the net in while the other took the fish from the net and put them into boxes.

As a general rule, the fishermen usually fished from the beginning of March until the end of November. The fishermen would haul their nets onto large reels to dry. So they would use one net one day while the other dried and Vice a Versa. The fishermen had a building close to the water which they called a "smack" where they would store their nets and other fishing equipment.

One year during Easter break Gary Cole (who was 14 years old at the time), along with four or five other young lads from Bowmanville Beach went out with Tom and Harry Depew and helped fish. They were fishing for Smelt which are now extinct on the Great Lakes. Smelt were around 10 inches long, and on an average day, the catch would number a thousand fish.

The Lighthouse Keepers

The Lighthouse, which exists on the West Beach today, is just a culvert standing on end and not a real lighthouse; it is merely a beacon which simply flashes and does not throw a beam out over the water. The original Darlington Harbor Company lighthouse was at the end of the pier on the east side of the harbour. It was a 20-foot long house with an attached tower with a revolving light on top. The light originated from a kerosene lamp and refractive mirrors. This light sent a beam out over the lake to help prevent possible shipwrecks.

Over the years, there were two prominent lighthouse keepers, and their names were: Tom Orr and Tom Norton. Tom Norton lived in a house just south of the railroad tracks where the Bowmanville and Soper Creeks merge. Just above his home where the 401 Highway crosses the creek, there was an island named Norton's Island, and it was named after Tom's family.

Tom Orr the other lighthouse keeper lived on East Beach and he has a dramatic story to tell. Tom died on the job after the lighthouse received a tremendous lightning strike one night. Auntie Robinson (a prominent old-time beach resident) often told an exciting piece of West Beach folklore. She said that when Tom Orr's body was discovered in the lighthouse, that he had been knocked entirely out of his boots. Rumours persist that when found, Tom's boots were still laced up. The lighthouse was so severely damaged by the lightning strike that the Darlington Harbour Company removed the attached house and simply replaced the tower with a lower replacement.

In the winter of 1938/1939, a significant winter storm blew the Lighthouse down, and it was last seen disappearing below the waves into the murky depths of Lake Ontario. The lighthouse was not rebuilt, although the fishermen from the beach put a metal hook at the end of the pier, and when they would go out to fish at night, they would hang a lantern on it to guide them back home again after completion of their work. In the 1960s, the government put up the beacon that is still there.

Lighthouse

The Boarding House

Mr. Berry built the main Boarding House on West Beach, as a two-story white frame structure around 1910. Mr. Berry was a well known Bowmanville merchant who ran the Berry Book Store near the corner of Division and King St. E. on the south side. Mr. Berry's daughter Novelda worked at the Boarding House in the summer and the bookstore in the winter. On the ground floor, there was a large screened veranda, a living room, a dining room, complete with a grand piano and a kitchen area, and there were sleeping quarters for the help. Upstairs was another screened veranda and about fourteen small rooms for the borders. Next door in the cottage now owned by Gary Cole, there were quarters for excess male boarders who took their meals in the main boarding house.

Across the back yard of the boarding house, there was a very long building with six compartments used as toilets. During the 1930s, a widow Mrs. Cecil Gatchell was the live-in cook/housekeeper at the Boarding House. She had two sons: Tom and Stan living with her. Mr. Berry was the owner/manager, while his daughter Novelda ran the store. Mrs. Gatchell's son Tommy ended up with a reasonably good job in the office of the Goodyear Rubber Company. Stanley joined the RCMP in 1948 and was sent to Nova Scotia. Charlie Severs bought the Boarding House, but it was starting to get into disrepair. Times finally overtook it, and it started getting pretty rustic.

Many of the borders (who came every weekend and for their holidays) were women who worked as Bell Telephone Company operators out-of Toronto. They got a package deal from Mr. Berry. Every weekend on Friday evening during the summer, a flotilla of rowboats would meet the Bell Telephone ladies at the Honey Bridge near the CNR station and row them down to the West Beach Boarding House. Again on Sunday night, the boats would return the girls to the CNR train station for their return trip back to Toronto. Mr. Berry for the most part kept the young men and the young women separate. Almost all the young men stayed at the other Boarding House next door.

In 1946 Mr. Berry sold the Boarding House complex to Charlie Severs, who, after two years, turned it into three summer apartments and then unexpectedly tore it all down. Out of the scrap, lumber Charlie Severs built the cottage that belonged to George Conlin and his family for many years (this cottage was also used for storage by the Port Darlington Harbor Company for many years). In more recent times, it has been common to refer to the Boarding House as: "The Port Darlington Sands Hotel." While this would have been a great name, it was never officially used while the Boarding House was in operation. What a shame as the Boarding House was the most prominent business on West Beach. It brought tourists to the beach area from all over. The name "Port Darlington Sands Hotel would have added a "just a bit of class" to our area.

In the back of the boarding house was a large six compartment outdoor toilet for the borders to use, as there was no indoor plumbing to speak of at that time except for one pump in the boarding house. The bedroom walls did not reach all the way up to the ceiling, so privacy was not guaranteed. The rooms were small, four feet by eight feet, just enough room for a cot and a wash-stand.

The origin of the name Honey Bridge came from the early days of the cottages. All cottages had a holding tank for their outdoor toilets, the waste from these would be pumped out into a container on a truck called a Honey Wagon. A sanitation worker used to come twice a week and remove what was referred to as the night soil. The gentleman who owned the Honey Wagon would take its contents and dump them into the creek at the same location as the creek bridge; hence, the name "Honey Bridge." If truth be known this story is a rumour, and no one knows if it is actually factual. Rowboats would pick up people who came to stay at the West Beach Boarding House and other cottages at the CNR station. They then would be rowed down the creek to West Beach, a rowboat ride which probably had an unmistakable aroma.

On May 24th., 1948, Mr. Berry sold the Boarding House to Gary Cole's uncle Charlie Severs. After he bought the Boarding House, he had a huge banquet and invited everyone on the beach to a turkey sit down dinner. Since the dining room and living room could only seat 20 people, three or four separate sittings were required to serve the meal. For this dinner banquet Gary Cole's mother, grandmother and aunts all cooked the supper. After the feast, there was a firecracker display. The banquet was one of the most significant events in West Beach history, and it was discussed for many years afterwards.

Gary's Uncle Charlie Severs could be a very complex character, he could be very abrupt but never held a grudge or at least not for long, and he also had a heart of gold, helping anyone who needed it. Charlie Severs also owned the Dancehall, and he was known as "Mr. West Beach."

Later, Mr. Severs turned The Boarding House into three separate apartments, which he would rent out for the summer. People wanted to spend their vacations up north in the Muskokas, Halliburton and the Kawartha region. At that time, people wanted more up-to-date facilities for their summer vacations, and so they stopped coming to the Boarding House, and as a result, Mr. Severs had it torn down around 1950.

Ther Boardinghouse had numerous antiques. Unfortunately, they were all destroyed or thrown away. In those days, people didn't understand the value of antiques. Mr. Severs instructed Gary Cole and his cousin to smash all the chamber pots and basins from each room and throw them into the garbage. Charlie Severs took the grand piano, from the Boarding House and placed it in the lake and used it as a dock for his boat, not being aware of its value.

Charlie Severs would offer people a package for the summer from the 24th of May to Thanksgiving weekend, and you could come and stay every weekend as well as your two weeks of vacation time and it was this offer that the Bell Telephone operators took advantage of. He also offered weekend and week-long packages to people. Charlie Severs had a cottage built from the torn Boarding House lumber. The first occupants of this cottage were a family named Chambers. Harry Chambers came to West Beach from Nova

Scotia with his wife and his four children: Vern, Harry Jr., Barbara, and a younger son Jackie and they lived in the cottage year-round.

Charlie Severs, sold the cottage to George Conlin and had it made into two cottages. George Conlin lived in one cottage, and his brother Frank lived in the other, later Frank decided he was going to sell his half of the cottage and George bought Frank's side and made it into one cottage again.

Mr. Berry's Boarding House

The Dancehall and General Store

The west part of the Dancehall had initially been a small cottage that belonged to a Scottish family named Grant. They always flew the yellow and red Rampant Lion of Scotland flag over their cottage. One year Mr. Grant returned alone to Scotland for a holiday, and Mrs. Grant refused to raise their flag until she received confirmation of her husband's safe arrival in the old country.

It was in the time frame of WWI that George "Joe" Dilling bought the Grant cottage and turned it into a general store. He extended the building on two different occasions to make it into what became the Dancehall. The building was narrow and long, and it ran perpendicular to the lake and oriented towards the river.

During the time that Mr. Dilling owned the Dancehall, there was no dancing allowed on Sundays. The general store which he ran was quite extensive because West Beach was, for the most part, isolated and difficult to access. The husbands of most beach families during the summer left during the week to go to their workplaces, while the wives and children stayed all week at their cottages. This made the General Store all that much more important. When the dance hall first opened, it was a time before nickelodeons and jukeboxes so Mr. Dilling had a small orchestra play instead. Dick Wedicomb and Ina McNaughton (Frank Pethick's piano playing daughter) were in the band. In those days, the dancehall routine was that it was the boy's responsibility to buy a ticket for each dance and afterward, he could ask the girl of his choice to have a dance. Frank Bottrell was the person responsible for collecting the dance tickets from the boys. Mr.

Dilling ran the Dancehall up to approximately 1946. Mrs. Dilling "Louie" Joe's wife ran a very tight ship at the Dancehall, and there was absolutely no hanky-panky allowed.

Since there was no road to West Beach at that time, all of Mr. Dilling's General Store supplies had to be delivered from town to the East Beach by Archie Tate. Joe would bring the supplies across the river to the West Beach by rowboat and, he also ran a small ferry across.

In front of the Dancehall, Mr. Dilling, with the Beach Association, had a large log for people to sit along with swings, a teeter-totter, a trapeze and a slide installed for the children.

In 1946 the Dancehall was sold to Bruce Murchison and Norm Green, who had married into the Auntie Robinson family. They married Auntie's two nieces, and they ran the Dancehall for two years. Mr. Murchison brought many small toys into the store for the children to buy, and the kids thought that was pretty good. One Sunday when it was raining, the kids asked permission to go into the Dancehall and dance and keep dry. Mrs. Murchison said: "she'd have to check with the chief of police to make sure it was okay to dance on Sunday." Police Chief Sid Venton gave his okay, and from then on, dancing was a popular event on Sundays.

In the summer of 1946, as the soldiers came home from the war, two songs were trendy, and they were played over and over in the Dancehall. They were: "The Roving Kind, She had a Dark and a Roving Eye" by the Weavers and "Flower of Malaya, Rose Rose I Love You" by Frankie Laine. In the summer of 1948, Gary Cole's uncle Charlie Severs bought the Dancehall, and he installed pinball machines, and even a one-armed bandit. It was at this time that the beach road opened, and many young people from the town of Bowmanville came to the beach to dance in the hall.

Charlie Severs and his wife, Irene, were very popular with the young people. His mother would walk up to Cedar Crest and stop at every cottage to ask if any groceries were needed from the general store. Edith Servers would then go to the telephone and call Charlie, who worked in General Motors in Oshawa and gave him the list. Charlie would stop on the way home and pick up what was needed and deliver it right to the door of each cottage.

Charlie and Irene ran the general store and Dancehall for approximately ten years until around 1955, eventually, though the general store grocery business started to peter out. Charlie was a good guy, but you didn't want to cross him because he had a wicked temper, although he never held a grudge. Charlie was well-liked by the people on the beach, and on Sports Day, he would give a free popsicles to all the children.

Every year the Sea Cadets from Toronto would come to the beach and camp-out in pup tents on the sand. During the Sea Cadets' visit, if it happened to rain, Charlie would tell them it was okay to come up and sleep on the Dancehall's floor. Eventually, Charlie sold the Dancehall and general store to Richard "Dutch" Butler (who was a Milkman in Oshawa) and his wife Evelyn and their daughter Susie. Mr. Butler would let the Beach Association show movies in the Dancehall on Saturday nights. One of the most popular films shown at the Dancehall was The Three Bears, and there was a new episode almost every week. Many of the movies were about travel, but there were also Hopalong Cassidy and The Three Stooges. During the summer Mr. Butler also held three adult dance parties including one on Sports Day. The invitation to these dance parties asked everyone to BYOB as many as 50 or 60 people attended. They also had a masquerade dance party where everyone dressed up in a costume, and one time they even had to square dance party. Mr. and Mrs. Butler were excellent people and were very popular with the people on the beach. The Butlers ran the Dancehall for approximately five years.

The next owners were two fellows by the name of Claire Jacobs and Don Babcock, and they would allow the Beach Association to have their meetings in the Dancehall on Sunday afternoons. Jacobs and Babcock had a Christmas theme dance party each year, where each guest was asked to bring a wrapped Christmas gift to put under the tree. Babcock worked in the Whitby psychiatric hospital, and he would take the gifts there to give to the patients.

On a personal note, Gary Cole, who is admittedly is a mediocre dancer, once had the opportunity to dance with a special girl when they were alone together in the Dancehall. She was about 16 years old and seven years younger than Gary. This girl was mature for her age, being tall and beautiful with long blond hair, and Gary considered her the most beautiful girl on Bowmanville Beach. On the day in question, she came to Gary in the

Dancehall and asked him to dance. Gary had to confess: "he'd very much like to dance with her, but he had never learned how to dance." Gary still sees this lady from time to time, and when he does, he tells her, "You know I still don't know how to dance." It's fun to speculate how things might have turned out different if Gary had danced with her that day.

Children in front of the Dancehall Joe Dilling with Vest & Fedora Hat

West Beach Dancehall

The Ice Houses

Behind the Dancehall, there were two wooden buildings which were called the Ice Houses. They were used to store ice for the cottage's iceboxes year-round. The ice houses were built by Joe Dilling and ice, cut from the marsh in the winter was stored there, in sawdust to act as insulation, and as a child, Gary Cole can remember playing in all that sawdust. Joe Dilling also used the ice to keep the soda pop sold in the Dancehall cold. The use of the ice houses became less necessary when the Williams Ice Company of Bowmanville began to deliver ice, door-to-door on the beach. Ice delivery became possible after the permanent road to the beach was opened. Charlie Severs removed the larger ice house in about 1948 and, Mr. Severs built public toilets, on the site of the larger icehouse, for the use of visitors. These toilets were also later removed. The smaller ice house was then used as a storage shed but was eventually also removed by Dutch Butler in 1955.

For a long time after the ice houses were no longer in use, the ice cutting and handling tools such as the big crosscut saw (with a handle on only one end) the ice tongs, and the mechanism used to score the end of the block of ice for splitting were still stored there. Joe Dilling also stored Kerosene in the ice houses and cottage owners on the beach could go to his store to buy Kerosene for their lamps and stoves etc.

Famous Families of Bowmanville Beach

Growing up on Bowmanville Beach was like growing up in a small Ontario village. Many of the same families lived on the beach for 70 years, resulting in interpersonal relationships existing among them. In many cases, guys and girls from different families would intermarry, and often guys would marry the girl next door. Families listed here are the beach residents who lived there the longest and entwined with each other the most.

The Dilling Family:

The Dillings were perhaps the foremost family on Bowmanville Beach, for most of its existence and had several branches.

George "Joe" Dilling was the man who built and owned the Dancehall; for the first 50 years he was "Mr. West Beach." George Dilling along with his wife Louise (AKA "Miss Louie") built the building that would become the Dancehall around 1910 and enlarged it several times. They had an apartment in the back of the Dancehall where they lived with their son Rance in the summertime. Rance was an avid sailboat enthusiast, who later owned a cottage on Crystal Beach. Rance had three daughters: Rena, Sandy, and Donna and a son named Bartholomew (AKA Jim an old-time Dilling name). Since the Dancehall kept him busy during the summer, Joe Dilling, wasn't able to ply his house painting trade. Although during the winter he did a lot of indoor painting work. Joe's older brother Herb Dilling was also a house painter who did a lot of outside work because he was available during the summer. Herb had five children, Ray, Lloyd, Forest, Nina, and Lena. Herb had two cottages on the beach, Sunnyside, and Linger Longer.

In approximately 1940 Forest bought Linger Longer cottage. He lived there with his wife Lillian, and their two sons: Wallace and Gary (both sailboat enthusiasts) and their daughter Catherine (often called Cookie). Forest was involved in bird banding, flying airplanes, local history and the Bowmanville Museum. The Dillings were related by marriage to Bill Barry, the owner of the Boarding House and he had one daughter named Novelda who was a cousin of the Dillings. The Dillings lived on Bowmanville Beach from 1900-1970, and they contributed as much or more to the beach as any other family.

The Fowler Family:

The Fowlers came from the Danforth area of Toronto, and Thomas Fowler built a cottage on Bowmanville Beach in 1915 which was later called the Irma Dell. Mr. Fowler's son, Alf, owned an import-export business In Toronto and since the Fowler's had such a large extended family, they didn't need many other people around. On the weekend it wasn't unusual to have 20 or more people in Irmadell. Alf Fowler had two daughters, Irma "Toots" (she married Ralph Redman). Ralph and Irma had three children: Joan, Doug and Ann). Alf's other daughter Shirley never married and at 96 still owns the cottage today and stays all summer. Alf Fowler's wife Gertie and her family also came to the cottage; along with Gertie's brother Ab Lowe and his wife Normie and their son Bob. Bob still goes to the cottage each year where he looks after the cottage chores for 96-year-old Shirley. Mrs. Ruby Benneyworth was the sister of Mrs. Gertrude Fowler. Ruby lived in Nashville, Tennessee where she was a receptionist at the Andrew Jackson Hotel. She knew all the country and western stars of the day that performed at the Grand Ole Opry, from Hank Snow to Elvis Presley, to Conway Twitty. Ruby enjoyed two or three weeks on Bowmanville Beach each summer. She brought autographed pictures of the country and western stars for the beach children.

Ruby had two sons: Walter and Albert (called Ab), they would spend their summers at the beach in the 1930s. Both Walter and Ab served in the American Air Force during WWII. Mrs. Fowler's other sister Irene Finlay (whose husband was a tinsmith in the city of St Catharines) also came down every summer. She would bring her children and her granddaughter Caroline Finlay. Irene cooked for all the Irmadell visitors and heaven help anyone who offered to help her prepare as the kitchen was hers and hers alone. Later members of the Fowler clan were: Bob Lowe and his daughter Stephanie,

Joan Redman and her two sons: Tim Knight and Murray Wilkinson, Doug Redman and his two daughters and Ann Redman. Ann was married to fellow beach resident Ron Parker, and they had a son Tyson Albert Parker. All of these fifth- generation Fowler family members have spent their summers at Irmadell.

The Latimer & Edwards Families:

The Latimer family had an interconnection with the Edwards family who had the cottage behind their cottage. Bert Latimer received the cottage from his aunt, Margarie Cameron and he had it rebuilt and moved to the north. Bert, a WWI veteran, married Dory Edwards (who lived with her mother, Annie "Granny" Edwards). Dory lived in the cottage behind theirs, and they had two daughters: Velda and Zetta. Velda married Bob MacLeish, and they had two daughters: Carol Anne and Alexandra. Zetta married Len Rider, and they had three children: Steve, Doug, and a daughter Sydney. Of the three, Sydney has kept in contact with the beach community and is still a frequent visitor.

The Edwards lived next door to the Latimer family in the cottage (called Welcome Inn) or more commonly known as: "Granny's." The Edwards (an English family) consisted of Mrs. Annie "Granny" Edwards, her daughter Dory Latimer and her sons Bert (who survived a gas attack at the 2nd Battle of Ypres during WWI) and Alf who was in the Royal Navy during WWI and WWII. He later became a Chief Petty Officer in the Royal Canadian Navy. The Latimer and the Edwards families were involved in the West Beach from its very earliest days and contributed significantly to make it what it was and what it still is today.

The Street & Matthews Families:

Bill and Ruby Street came from the Danforth area of Toronto, where Bill was a janitor at a public school there. They had five children: Jean (who had a disability), Winifred, Madeline, Bill Jr. and Peggy. Winnifred married Jack Cully of Bowmanville, and they had three children: Marilyn, Bill and Marsha. Madeline married Jack Parker of Bowmanville they had two sons: David and Ron. Peggy married Ross Wright from Bowmanville, and they had one son, Tom and three daughters Joy, Nancy and Robin. Both Winnifred and Madeline later owned cottages on West Beach.

Coming from Toronto and originally from Cork Ireland, Mr. Matthews served in WWI. He and his wife Flossie had two children: a son Andy and a daughter Betty. The Matthews had a connection to the Street family. Betty married Lionel Parker, the younger brother of Jack Parker and they had three children: sons Paul and Doug and daughter Mary. Like the Latimers, the Street and Matthews families made significant contributions to West Beach.

The Robinson Family:

This large family with many branches and intersections and headed by Miss Edith Robinson owned three different cottages on West Beach. Edith was the matriarch of the family and who everyone called "Auntie." She had two nieces and a nephew (her sister's children) and their surname was White, and they would spend their summers at the beach. Their given names were: Don, Dorothy and Marion. Don later lost interest in the beach and eventually drifted away from it. Marion (AKA Marnie) married Bruce Murchinson whose parents had a cottage on the beach.

They had two sons: Bill and Peter and they later had a cottage up on Crystal Beach. Dorothy married a fellow named Norman Green, who was a carpenter at the Simpsons department store in Toronto. They also owned a cottage on Crystal Beach, and they had two children: Don and Marylou. Auntie was a practical nurse who looked after ill and disabled people. At one time Auntie owned a boarding house for university and college students in Toronto. Auntie Robinson was like a stepmother to Peggy Kelly who also spent her summers at the West Beach cottage. Peggy married Norm Jake Mulholland from Bowmanville, and they had three children. Their children were: Gail (who married Chuck MacDonald and they had a son: Brent Hooey) and Karen (who married Harvey Greenley and had two daughters: Kelly and Cassie) and son Howard who never married.

Right next door to Robinsons was the Bakewell family cottage. Beatrice Bakewell (whose maiden name was White) was the sister of the guy who married Auntie's Robinson's sister. Beatrice White worked at a large cafeteria in Toronto, and she married a guy named Claire Bakewell, and for a time they had a cottage on Crystal Beach. In the 1930s, Claire Bakewell and his son Bruce built the cottage Cliff View (AKA The Hutch) which is still there today. They had a daughter named Lorna who married Bert Hutchinson from Cove Road. They had two daughters: Judy and Sharon. Judy became a school teacher in Toronto and married a school principal named Alec Ginou, and they had one daughter: Lindsay. Sharon worked for an insurance company, and she married Jack Eccles, and they had one child: Corey. Sharon is now married to Ross Smith and is the grandmother of Corey's son Tristan Eccles.

This large and prominent West Beach family is still present on the beach. Gail and Chuck MacDonald, as well as Sharon and Ross Smith, still maintain cottages on the beach.

The Cole Family:

The Cole Family originally bought a cottage on Bowmanville Beach around 1940. Their first connection with Bowmanville Beach was through Gary Cole's great-grandfather, Sam Cole and his wife Martha (nee Goode). Sam was a day labourer, and he fought hard to support his wife, three sons and two daughters.

Sam and Martha lived in an old house in the South Ward of Bowmanville which belonged to Martha's father. Sam's connection to Bowmanville Beach was during the times that he fished and trapped muskrats there during the 1890s long before the building of any cottages. During this time Sam lived in a tent pitched on the sand of Bowmanville Beach. One damp and cold spring, Sam tragically caught pneumonia and died at around 35 years of age. Left with five children, Widow Martha Cole found things very difficult for the remainder of her life.

Gary father Fred Cole's first connection with West Beach was when he visited his uptown neighbour (Daddy Couch's) cottage for a swim. Named: "Camp Cozy" and situated on Crystal Beach; Fred swam with his friends: Bruce, Roy and Morgan Lunney. The Lunney boy's uncle and later their father also owned a cottage on Crystal Beach. Incidentally the youngest Lunney brother, "Jake" was the only person ever born on West Beach.

Around 1940 Gary Cole's grandmother Nora Cole, and his aunt Marg Cole bought the Bosky Dell cottage. Gary's parents: Edie and Fred would spend the summer there with Gary's grandmother and aunt. Previously Fred and Edie had rented a cottage up on the Cove Road for one summer. They didn't fancy Cove Road and so the next summer they came back and rented the right side of the Hallman cottage on Crystal Beach. Edie said she liked that cottage because there was a hole in the floor and she could sweep the sand down that hole and a dustpan wasn't required.

After that Edie and Fred would spend the next several summers at Bosky Dell and this is where Gary had his first experiences on the beach. It was here that Gary took his first steps as a 9-month-old toddler on the verandah of Bosky Dell. Gary always says, "I may not have been born on Bowmanville Beach, but I'm pretty sure I was conceived there." In 1941 Fred Cole bought the cottage known as the "Coal Hole" where he spent the rest of his summer years. Later on, Edie and Gary bought one of the cottages in the Boarding House complex and named it Rathkeale after a village in County Limerick Ireland. Gary's grandmother, Nora Delmage's father, came from Rathkeale Ireland.

Over time Gary's grandparents turned the Bosky Dell cottage over to Gary's uncle Walter and his wife, Dory. Walter, Dory and their son Merle had the cottage for many years. Gary's mother's maiden name was Severs, and around 1948 her brother Charlie Severs bought the Dancehall and then the Boarding House.

Charlie Severs and his wife Irene had two sons: Bill and Wayne. In those days Charlie was the: "Uncrowned King of the Beach." Later Gary's other grandfather Bill Servers Sr. and his wife Edith bought the Street family cottage and called it Pop's Place. After leaving the army around 1949, Gary's uncle Ben Severs built a cottage on the north side of the back road close to the marsh and close to Suzie Dunn's cottage. Ben Servers met his wife Jeanie in Newfoundland on his way overseas during WWII and married her there. They had three children: Kenny, Bobby and Marnie. Jeanie Servers still spends her summers in her present cottage which is the former Matthews cottage.

Another branch of the family was Clinton "Bud" Henning and his wife, Marion Hayes. Marion's mother Mary Hayes was the sister of Edie Cole (Gary's mother). The Hennings bought the old Carpenter cottage: "Rendezvous" and used it with their family for many years.

Interesting People & Events of Darlington West Beach

A fellow named Bill Carlton once built a lean-to shack near the end of Cove Road close to the 2nd Marsh. For one or two summers he sold pop, candy bars and hot dogs (called Carlton's Red Hots) out of his shack there. He had a kerosene stove with a pot of boiling water on it where he would warm-up his hot dogs. Quite often in the evening, a guy would walk his girlfriend, or a husband would walk his wife down to the shack and treat his gal to a hot dog. This practice was quite common, and so "Carlton's Red Hots" were very popular in those days.

There was another fellow by the name of Duckie Needs who built a little store called "Duckie's Winter Green." Located where the two creeks merged and close to where Mr. Depew kept his fishing nets. Duckie also rented out boats, and he sold candy bars, pop, hot dogs, hamburgers, coffee, as well as donuts. Many couples from Bowmanville frequented Duckies because canoes and rowboats were available for a romantic paddle on the river. For five or six years Duckie lived in the same building that he used for his business. Duckie rented the land for his business from a local farmer by the name of Mr. Short. Eventually, Duckie had to move to larger quarters located close to the Honey Bridge. At this new location, it was possible for folks to rent a motorboat and dock space and dew worms were also available. Inside, there was a table, chairs and a Nickelodeon; with enough room for a few couples to dance. When the hydro line went through, Duckie had to move again as it was unlawful to have a building located under hydro lines. Roy "Duckie" Needs at one time was also the manager of the old Bowmanville Arena. He also repaired radios as a side business, a skill he acquired while serving in the Canadian Air Force.

At this point, there was a marsh just above Cedar Crest, which was known as the 3rd marsh and AKA Hall's Marsh and The Breaker's Inn. There was a building there which was reported to have been one of the oldest buildings in Darlington Township. It belonged to the Burke family who were one of the original United Empire Loyalists pioneer families who arrived in this area from the United States. When Gary Cole was a young boy, the building belonged to the Simmons family, and they ran it as a boarding house. Mr. Simmons had married one of the Burke girls, and as result, he was able to acquire the farm. There was a milk stop at Maple Grove for the train, and in those days it was possible to catch the train there if you were able to flag it down. Mr. Simmons would pick up his borders at the Maple Grove milk stop and drive them down to his boarding house. Commonly referred to as Simmon's Boarding House; the correct name turned out to be "The Breakers Inn." This information came from a fellow who had married one of the Simmons' granddaughters.

On the hill above Breakers Inn, there was a land formation called Raby Head. In 1866 a man galloped into Bowmanville on horseback warning everybody that: "the Fenians are coming." Apparently the Fenians had been spotted at Halls Marsh, and the town was at risk of invasion. Promptly the militia formed a defensive picket line along the Bowmanville Creek. Although no Fenian attack ever happened.

During WWI in 1916, Norm Bottrell reported a German submarine sighting off Hall's March. Norm was the father of a friend of 15- year-old Gary Cole, and Norm went there to determine the sighting's authenticity but found nothing.

Many years ago, a fellow from Brockville by the name of Frederick Knapp invented a new type of boat which he named: "The Roller- Boat." The inventor eventually formed a business partnership with a local Bowmanville daredevil-performer who called himself "The Great Farini" who on August 15th, 1860 walked a tight rope across Niagara Falls. His real name was William Hunt, and his father was the Reeve of Bowmanville at the time. Knapp and Hunt met up on the Toronto waterfront aboard the Roller-Boat and set out with their destination being Prescott Ontario. They soon ran into troubles though as they had miscalculated how much coal they would need to complete the journey. Without fuel, the boat soon washed ashore at

Mann's Point also known as Raby Head, which is the highest point on Lake Ontario east of the Scarborough Bluffs. On top of Mann's Point was a big house called Raby Cottage and the Roller-Boat was no doubt observable from that location, floundering in the waves of Lake Ontario. Knapp and Hunt were able to get into Bowmanville and purchase some coal for the boat's steam engine and eventually completed their voyage to Prescott. The high expectations of the legendary Roller-Boat, in the end, unfortunately, turned out to be a colossal failure. Towed back to Toronto Harbour, the Roller-Boat became the source of numerous lawsuits. It sat for many years, and rumours have it that it is now buried under the Gardiner Expressway desolate and long forgotten.

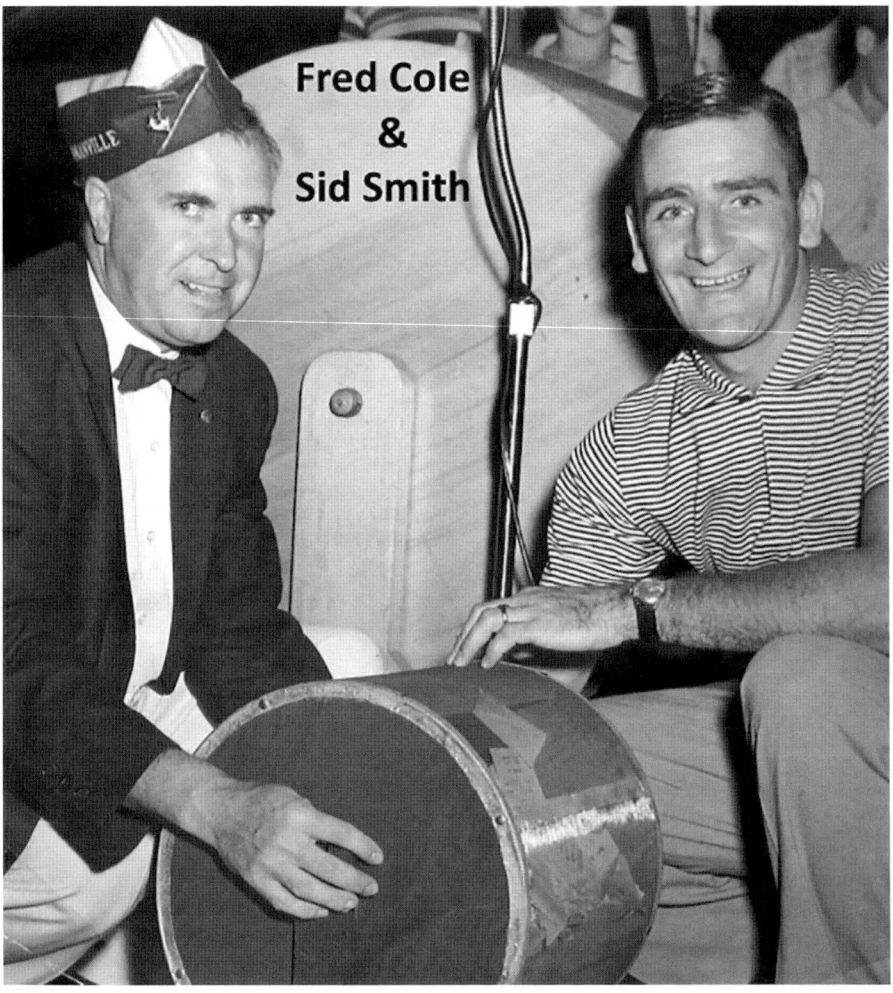

Fred Cole & Sid Smith

Trudy Young

Mrs. Fox Gate

Access to Bowmanville West Beach years ago was complicated. Initially, the road only went a little bit south of the Honey Bridge. It was not a legal railway crossing and was only a farmer's road.

Since only the farmer could legally cross there, the beach was isolated, and the only way to access the beach was to walk. When people started building cottages on the West Beach, the only way to access their cottage was to drive to East Beach and take a boat across the river to West Beach. As the beach started to develop the cottagers developed the road more and extended it further toward the lake. The roadway extension to the cottages and the backroad was put in during the early 1920s. The roadway after the Honey Bridge down to approximately where the conservation area is today went through Mrs. Fox's property. The Fox Family owned the entire Cove which they had bought from the farmer. In the early 20s and 30s, the Fox's sold several lots. Almost everybody who lived on the Cove came from Toronto, and they were mostly Baptists which was pretty well unknown around Bowmanville at that time. Sometime in the early 1930s, Mrs. Fox put a gate across the road where it entered her property. The people who lived in the Cove had a key to the lock on the gate.

They could come through, but nobody else could.

At the south end of the road where it bends, Mrs. Fox had a six- foot-wide and two feet deep trench dug to stop the flow of traffic. Sometime in the 1930s Mrs. Fox and the other cottage owners on the Cove built a causeway across the 2nd marsh, and this allowed the people who lived on the Cove to come via Waverly Road and across the Cedar Crest Road. This causeway was of low quality and it gave way to a springtime flood in the mid-1930s which washed it out. To rectify the problem of the West Beach cottagers not being able to get into their cottages, the Port Darlington Harbor commission supplied a ferry which went across the harbour, although it was little more than a scow. Operated by the Colmer brothers of Bowmanville it was ferried across the harbour by hand with a rope, and carried only one car at a time. A problem arose in the late summer when the river's harbour water level dropped. This water level drop made it challenging to get the cars off the ferry on to the West Beachside. The car ferry was named the Mary Ann after the daughter of James McClellan who ran the Darlington Harbour Company.

Tom Ross, who owned the Royal movie theatre in town, was quite a community-conscious type of guy, and he built and paid for a road which was to the east of Mrs. Fox's road. By using this road, the cottagers could outflank Mrs. Fox's Road. All of the road access foolishness caused a lot of hard feelings among the cottage community. One Sunday morning, when the Cove cottagers woke up, they found Mrs. Fox's ditch full of garbage.

One year the causeway washed out, and the cove cottagers had to access their cottages from the main road from Liberty Street. Mrs. Fox then relented and let the West Beach people drive through. Every year the West Beach Cottage Association had to send a letter to Mrs. Fox asking to use the road, and she would send a message back saying whether it was okay or not.

Eventually, the town of Bowmanville bought Mrs. Fox's section of the roadway which then became the main thoroughfare to get into the cottages. Why Mrs. Fox caused all the fuss in the first place no one knows, the cottage owners were, for the most part, kind and decent people and weren't causing her any harm.

The Railway Crossing – West Beach as a Gated Community

Originally the railway crossing was a place where the local farmer could cross the train tracks; no one else could legally use it. Over the years, as more people came and built their cottages on West Beach, they started to cross over the railroad tracks also. The Grand Trunk Railway (later the CNR) said that for safety reasons, the beach residents could no longer cross. The Beach Association, at the time, petitioned the railroad to allow the cottagers the use of the crossing. An agreement was reached and it stipulated that a crossing guard was required in July and August. As a result, the Beach Association hired three men to guard the crossing. A small shack on the south side of the crossing offered the guards a place to relax and get shelter from the elements.

In the shack, there was a wood stove, a small cot, and a table and chair. The on-duty guard would receive a schedule showing when the trains would be coming. In the daytime, the guard would come out and close the gate on the south side. The approach to the tracks on the south side was steep, and the visibility was poor. As the train approached, the guard then stood on the north side with a red flag warning approaching motorists that a train was approaching. After the train had gone by, the guard would open the gate, and everybody could go safely through. In the evening and night-time, the guard held a red lantern instead of the flag.

Over the years, there were three guards: Bill Dunn (who lived on the beach), George Buttonshaw (who lived a short distance away in the South Ward), and Gordon Moorcroft, who lived in the town. Gordon had lost parts of both of his hands in an accident while he was working at Goodyear Plant. Dunn and Buttonshaw did the day shift while Moorcroft did the night shift. This arrangement carried on until the 401 came through in the 1950s. At that time, a new road & crossing were built to allow safer access to the beach.

The Beach Association

The Bowmanville West Beach Association got its start around 1919 and coordinated itself later into the Civic Holiday and the annual Sports Day events. Raising money to pay for the beach services such as the railway/gate guards and the sanitation workers were the Beach Association's primary purpose.

The presidents of the Beach Association over the years were, Edwin Lattrell, Bruce Murchison, Abe Lowe, Gary Cole's father Fred, and Len Rider. Len was the president for the last 5-10 years until the association went dormant. Len Ryder's main claim to fame was that he was a dead ringer for US President John F. Kennedy. The joke around the beach was that if Len had been in Dallas, Texas, on November 22, 1963, President Kennedy would have likely been able to serve out his term. Lillian Dilling was the long-term Secretary of the Beach Association, and Forest Dilling was the treasurer of the beach Association for many years. Gary Cole's father, Fred, was the long-serving and dedicated treasurer of the association for quite a while, as was Walter Cole and Donnie Masters. The treasurer's position was probably the beach association's most thankless although essential job. Each spring, it was the treasurer's job to go around to each cottage and collect the $10 to $15 membership fee. Human nature being what it is, some cottagers weren't fond of taking their wallets out of their pockets. On some occasions, the treasurer had to call back two, three or more times.

Weekly euchre tournaments were held as fund raisers by the beach association and each week with new matches being held in different cottage locations. Gary Cole's aunt Ella Currie was the main organizer of the euchre tournaments for many years. The rules were that if your cottage hosted the tournament that week, you would be responsible for supplying the lunch. Lunch typically consisted of a loaf of buttered fruit bread and tea. Usually, one or two tables of players would arrive from the Southward. After travelling to East Beach by taxi, Mr. Dilling would row them across the river. Afterwards, they would be rowed back across, and a cab would bring them home again. Gary Cole's aunt would collect and carry several card tables and chairs, setting them up in the host cottage of the week. These tournaments would raise two or three dollars a week for the beach association, which wasn't much but back in those days two or three dollars went a lot further than it does now. Back in those long distant days, folks did what they could to raise money, and they used their ingenuity and found ways to entertain themselves.

Sports Day

Sports day always held on the Civic holiday weekend. Years ago, it was quite a bit larger than it is now. Sports day originally started on West Beach in 1919 after the First World War, and at that time, they called it the Victory Sports Day. It was during this time of increased cottage building that the Beach Association was formed. The Beach Association ran the first Victory Sports day in 1919, the entire Town Council was invited and were served a meal on the beach.

The Beach Association's purpose was to make life better for the cottagers. Their purpose was also, to acquire services for the cottagers such as a guard at the gate. At the time the Beach Association was first formed, each cottage owner was required to pay $2.00 each in annual fees. Eventually, the Sports Day expanded to include the whole Civic holiday weekend. On Saturday, there would be a carnival on the beach with bingo, crown & anchor, spin the wheel for a basket of fruit, fish pond etc. In the old days, the West Beach carnival rivalled the uptown fairs such as those held by the Rotary Club and Lions Club. On Sunday, they had a sandcastle building contest and a treasure hunt for the children, which were run for many years by Forest Dilling and later by Gary Cole.

In later years a men's horseshoe contest was held on Sunday morning around 10 AM. The horseshoe contest was quite a significant event with between 80 and 100 players. In the early 1950s, Sid Smith, (captain of the Toronto Maple Leafs) and West Beach cottage owner ran the horseshoe contest. The rules of the horseshoe contest were that after picking partners, everyone paid $1, and if you lost, you were eliminated from the competition. At 5:00 Sunday afternoon, there was a dress-up parade for the children. Each costumed child would parade up and down the beach. In later years Gary Cole would bring a few of his pipe band buddies from the Legion, and they would lead the children who were participating in the parade up and down the beach.

Afterwards, prizes for the best children's costume were presented. It was always quite a big event, and the children always looked forward to it. Judy Hutchison, who was a baton twirler with the Toronto Leaside Lions, led the parade in her majorette costume and baton. After the ceremony was over on Sunday night, there was a concert, and this was the most popular event for the people who attended Sports Day.

During most of the 1930s and 1940s, the concert organizer was Mrs. Eleanor Durno (who owned Cheerio cottage). Eleanor was an employee of the Toronto Telegram newspaper, and the paper had an entertainment group during World War II to entertain the soldiers and raise funds to help the war effort. Eleanor was the head of this entertainment group, which she called the Cheerios. This group is where the name of her cottage originated. Eleanor's group consisted of 10 to 12 people, including several Bowmanville boys such as Glenn Virtue, Paddy Welsh and other people who played the guitar. Nina Creamer (who eventually bought Cheerio cottage) was the lead female singer in the group. There was also a visually impaired accordion player in the group; who sang a viral song about a goat that went to Berlin during the Second World War and spat in the Fuehrer's face. This song was a great favourite with the crowd, with everyone joining in the chorus. The Cheerio group provided professional entertainment at the concert, although any cottager or their children who had talent from singing or playing a musical instrument or tap dancing could also volunteer to entertain the crowd. Four boys from Tennessee spent the summer on West Beach, and Mrs. Durno would train them to perform a skit each year. These lads would rehearse in Eleanor's cottage for a week before the concert. One-year, she had the boys dress up as pirates, and this was a big hit at the show. A big stage was erected in front of the Dancehall and a piano was brought out onto the stage to be used during the concert. Two or three hundred people would attend the concert; sitting on the sand or on lawn chairs.

Around 1950 Mrs. Durno retired from running the concert, and Gary Cole's mother, Edie Cole, successfully replaced her. During this time, the people who played the piano were, Mrs. Gertrude Hallman, Ella Curry, Mrs. Iris

Cooper, and Mr. George Young. Mr. Young had been a pianist in England with the Royal Air Force marching band. There were also square dancing and Mr. Young's daughter Trudy (who became a professional dancer and movie star in Toronto) entertained, along with fellow cottager and concert entertainer Mary Lou Green.

Every year at the concert, a beauty contest for men in drag added to the fun. Edie Cole's found out that her neighbour Bert Edwards secretly wanted to take part of the show but had not been asked. When Edie found out about Bert's desire to participate she happily invited him to take part, he jumped at the chance. Bert happily had his costume already prepared and was raring to go. As luck would have it, Bert, not only participated in that year's beauty concert but he won 1st prize. Bert Edwards had been in the first world war and had done some pantomime to entertain the troops. This experience had served him well during the beauty pageant in drag, and he ended up as the hit of the show. One year, men were asked to dress up as Hawaiian dancers at a luau.

Participants in this fun show were: Len Rider, Milt Corson, Sid Smith, and Jack Parker.

Another year a mock wedding was held where the girls dressed as the men and the men dressed as women. At the mock wedding ceremony, Gary Cole's father performed the duties of the minister. After the concert, a silver collection was taken up from the crowd to help pay for the expenses.

On the Monday of the Civic holiday weekend, the primary sports day would take place, and the first event was the running race for children five years and younger. Regardless of what position each child finished in the race, each child received a prize. There were also races for boys and girls up to 15 years old, and there were also mixed events. Another popular game was the shoe race, where the girls took off their shoes and put them in a pile at the end of the race and the boys had to run down and pick out their partner's shoes and then run back to where girls were and put the shoes on her feet, then run again to the end of the race in order to win. There were also wheelbarrow races which requiring participates to run one way, then switch positions and run back again. There were also potato sack races where the winner had to hop to the finish line inside a potato sack. Another was the piggyback race; each participant ran to the finish line with their partner on your shoulders. There were also adults sports such as the men's balloon competition where each participant had a balloon attached to his back, and the other man had to try to burst his opponent's balloon (this sometimes got rather violent). They also had the egg throwing contest where a man and his female partner had to throw a raw egg back and forth while taking one step backwards without breaking the egg. The last couple who still had their egg unbroken won the prize. The booby prize was that the winners had to break the egg over their partner's head to prove that it was not hard-boiled.

There were also water races in the lake or the Harbour. They had two people canoe races, rowboat races, and canoe jousting races where one person was paddling and the other with a long pole (padded at one end) attempted to knock an opponent off his canoe. The opponent tried to defend himself with a shield, such as a garbage can lid. Similar to the Knights of Old, the winner would be the last person still in his canoe standing. This event took place in the harbour, and the canoeing contestants started approximately fifty feet apart, this was a top-rated event. There were also swimming races across the harbour; in those days, the harbour was twice the width that it is today. One year Mr. Dilling set up an obstacle race where contestants had to swim around obstacles in the Harbour. Another competition was the tub race, where contestants had to paddle across the Harbour and a bath or laundry tub. There was also a dog race where contestants took their dogs to the east side of the Harbour and then the dogs raced across to the west side.

One year on Sunday, the Dr. Ballard dog food company came down to the beach and put on a dog show. Anybody on the beach who had a dog that could do a trick or was dressed up in a costume could enter. There were ten or twelve different events, and the winner in each got a prize. And anybody who was there with a dog got free cans of Dr. Ballard's dog food just for showing up.

On sports day a big raffle was also held where the prize was: a refrigerator or a television. One year sports day got rained out and had to held a week later. They held two additional events, and this caused a big sensation. The first other event was a real beauty contest with eight or nine young ladies.

The winner received the title Miss West Beach. The competition was open for anybody, and one girl from Oshawa, who was a professional model, won the contest. The judges were the president of the local service clubs, such as the Lions Club president Mr. Goddard, and the Kinsmen president. One contestant was Brenda Cooper, who was a resident of West Beach and a beautiful Judy Garland look-alike. Her number in the competition was number eight, and when her number didn't win, it caused an uproar. When announced that the girl from Oshawa was the winner, a fellow in the audience stood up and started yelling that number 8 (Brenda Cooper) should have won.

That same year in the afternoon, they had the most beautiful baby under a year of age contest. This contest took place and judged in Cole's family cottage, and there must have been 25 babies there. The judge of the competition was one of the most famous doctors that Bowmanville ever had, Dr. Howard Rundle who brought two nurses with him. This contest was not determined by how good-looking a baby was but by how healthy they were. All the babies were weighed and had their hearts tested and had their ears examined. Dr. Rundle stayed and had lunch, after which he said: "I'm going now and the nurses are going with me, And when you see my car cross the Honey Bridge, please announce the winner." The winner of the healthiest baby contest was Pearl Steiner, the daughter of a West Beach family who was originally from Toronto and lived in Moonshine Cottage

The Dancehall

Marion Henning Charlie Severs Edith Cole Chuck Ormsbee

Sports Day on the Beach

Horseshoes on the Beach
Civic Holiday

Civic Holiday 1955 Dancehall in background Kid's Dress-up

Joanie Redman, Dave Parker, Bob Lowe, Carol Ann Finley
Ron Parker, Bill Cully, Marilyn Cully,
Ann Redman, Cindy Rider,
Carol Ann McLeish.
Dancehall in Background

BOWMANVILLE BEACH ASSOCIATION

SPORTS DAY PROGRAM

Civic Holiday Weekend, 1964

SUNDAY, 1.00 P.M. —
Treasure Hunt, Boys and Girls, 12 and under .... 3 Prizes

1.30 P.M. —
Sand Castles, 4, 5, 6, 7 .... 2 Prizes
Sand Castles, 8, 9, 10 .... 2 Prizes

6.30 P.M. — Children's Dress-up Parade

9.00 P.M. — Concert

MONDAY, 10.30 A.M. —
Men's Horseshoe Pitching .... Prize to Winning Team

2.00 P.M. —
Tots Race, 5 and under .... Prizes for all
Girls Race, 6 and 7 .... 3 Prizes
Boys Race, 6 and 7 .... 3 Prizes
Girls Race, 8 and 9 .... 3 Prizes
Boys Race, 8 and 9 .... 3 Prizes
Ladies Spot Race .... 1 Prize
Girls Race, 10 and 11 .... 3 Prizes
Boys Race, 10 and 11 .... 3 Prizes
Men's Sack Race .... 1 Prize
Mixed Piggy Back Race, 14 and under .... 2 Prizes
Ladies' Shoe Kicking Contest .... 2 Prizes
Girls Sack Race, 15 and under .... 2 Prizes
Men's Spot Race .... 1 Prize
Girls Shoe Race, 12 and under .... 2 Prizes
Boys Piggy Back Race, 12 and under .... 2 Prizes
Mixed Couples Shoe Race, 16 and over .... 2 Prizes
Egg Throwing Contest, 14 and over .... 1 Prize
Boys Sack Race, 15 and under .... 2 Prizes
Egg Throwing Contest (Married Couples) .... 1 Prize
Girls' Swimming Race, 14 and under .... 2 Prizes
Boys' Swimming Race, 14 and under .... 2 Prizes
Swimming Race, 20 and under .... 2 Prizes

49

The Beach Services

The Honey Men

Bowmanville West Beach was like a small village, and as is the case in all communities, certain services were essential. One of these essential services was sewage disposal. At first all the cottages had pit toilets, and since the beach was all sand, this was not an ideal solution. People had to draw their drinking water and wash their clothes out of the same water. The Harbour Company deemed that this was not healthy. Eventually all the toilets were fitted with garbage cans to hold the waste. Men known as the honey men would come twice a week (Tuesdays and Saturdays) to pick up the waste and haul it away. The honey men were paid by the Beach Association, with each cottager paying $15.00 per year for the service. Over the years, the three honey men who serviced the beach were: "Skin" Clayton, and Harold "Hi" Raby (because Harold was 6' 6" he got the nickname: "Hi"). Harold used a horse and wagon to pick up the waste, and he would usually make his rounds in the evening. Another honey man was Howard Burgess. Howard worked at the Goodyear plant, but he was also the sanitation worker for all of Bowmanville. Rather than a horse and wagon, Howard used a truck, and he would pick up the night soil as well as the garbage and haul it up to the Bowmanville dump at Jackman Road. This arrangement carried on until around 1974 when the town took over all of the garbage collection.

The Icemen

In the early days of Bowmanville West Beach, a refrigerator had not yet been invented, nor was electricity available. As a result, the beach residents needed another way to refrigerate their food. During the 1920s and early 30s, the cooling of food had to be accomplished by the use of iceboxes and these ice boxes needed ice. Except for the Dancehall, there wasn't an electric refrigerator on West Beach until the early 1950s. West Beach residents bought their ice from Mr. Dilling (who owned the Dance Hall and the General Store). Mr. Dilling cut the ice in the winter from the marsh and stored it in sawdust in the ice houses. After the road to the beach was finalized in the late 1930s, the Williams Ice Company started delivering ice to each cottage door to door on Tuesdays, Thursdays and Saturdays. The Williams made their ice in an ice factory on King Street in Bowmanville, and Mr. Jimmy Williams owned the ice company. The delivery man who delivered the ice door to door was: Russ "Brownie" Brown. Mr. Williams also had two icemen helpers during those days, and their names were Clint Ferguson and Gary Cole. Even though Gary was only 12 years old at the time, he was carrying 50 lb blocks of ice. As time went by, and more people were getting electric refrigerators, the ice company eventually went out of business.

The Vegetable Delivery Man

Mr. Ernie Pasant (who worked at the Goodyear Plant), also ran a small market garden business on the corner of Duke Street and Baseline. On Saturday, during the growing season, he would come down to the beach with vegetables (carrots, beets, turnips, potatoes, etc.) and sell them door to door. Ernie's main claim to fame was that he also sold beautiful bouquets of gladiolus. During the summer, every cottage would have a beautiful bouquet of gladiolus on their front veranda. Mr. Pasant was a very well-liked and respected man on the beach.

The Postman

Bowmanville East Beach dancehall had a sub-post office, and people could have their mail delivered there. From there, Gary Cole picked it up and delivered it to the West Beach Dancehall and General Store, where people on West Beach could pick it up.

The Policeman

In the old days, each of Bowmanville's three Wards had their special police constables, including Bowmanville West Beach. At the time, Bowmanville's police force consisted of the police chief, Sidney Venton, who worked day shift and Walter "Fat" Hall, who worked the night shift. The special Ward Constables would only be on duty during special occasions like parades or to keep an eye on things on Halloween night etc. The South Ward Special Constable was Mr. Archie Matthews, who had a cottage on Crystal Beach. There was a framed wooden shack behind Mr. Couch's cottage named "Camp Cozy" which acted as a makeshift jail. It was also called, "The West Beach Lock Up." It measured eight feet by 8 feet and had a lock on the door. Crime on West Beach was virtually non-existent, and it is doubtful that anyone was ever locked up in it.

The Firemen

Bowmanville West Beach had its volunteer fire brigade. In the old days, Bowmanville had two Fire Halls, one on Church Street, which had a large pump wagon and one on Neilson Street for the Southward, which had a smaller pumper. There was a comical character in Bowmanville at that time by the name of Casey Martyn. He ran a livery stable in town, and he also owned the bowling alley on King Street East near Division St. At one time, Casey decided to start his own fire brigade, for which he bought a hand pumper. It was six or seven feet long and inside was a large reservoir for water and on each side was a handle to pump it. The hand-pulled pumper was painted red with: "Martyn's Fire Brigade" painted in gold letters on the side. Martyn's Fire Brigade eventually went out of business, and the hand pumper donated to the Bowmanville West Beach for their fire brigade. Around 1918 the Bowmanville West Beach fire brigade took the pumper to the river filled it up with water and with all the teenage boys from the beach pumping it, they could shoot water clear across the river to the other side. The pumper never saw use as there were never any significant fires in the cottages until more modern times.

The Ferry

There was a ferry on the river which was run by the Colmer brothers which could carry one car at a time from the East Beach to the West Beach. The ferry was a scowl, and it was named: "The Mary Ann" by the president of Port Darlington Harbour Company, Mr. James McClellan, after his daughter. Gary Cole never actually saw the ferry in service, but he did see its remains tied up behind Fred Depew's fish dock. Its operation consisted of a windlass, where two men would stand side by side and turn the windlass, and a rope would carry the ferry across the river.

Ferry scow tied to the dock

Ferry Scow & Coal Sheds

The Beach at War

The sports day on the beach began as the Victory Sports Day in 1919, following the conclusion of WWI.

On June 6th, 1944, Gary Cole's mother, along with her neighbour, Mrs. Parker, would sit on the porch of their cottage listening to the news reports on the radio concerning the troops landing on D- Day. Gary Cole's mother's brother Ben Severs, and Mrs. Parker's husband Jack were both part of the D-Day invasion.

During World War II, somebody came up with the idea that they could make rubber out of the sap of the milkweed plant. Mr. Ross, who was the owner of the Royal Theater in Bowmanville, enlisted the help of the children of Bowmanville to pick as much milkweed as they could and deliver it to him. The person who collected the most substantial amount of milkweed earned a prize of a catcher's baseball mitt, and Wallace Dilling from the beach won it. Mr. Ross also devised a plan to recycle empty tin cans to help with the war effort, and if a child brought 2 or 3 tin cans, he or she would be given free admission to the movie theatre matinee on Saturdays. In August 1945, during the VJ Day celebrations, the cottagers had a conga line going, which went in one door of each cottage and out the other. Everybody was singing the song "Happy Days Are Here Again." On that day, Gary Cole went into the Dilling cottage, and there was a dummy in a chair dressed as Hirohito the 124th Emperor of Japan. Later this dummy was taken down to the river in front of the Cheerio cottage, where they had a huge bonfire, and they burned the emperor at the stake.

Although Bowmanville Beach was a small community, there were a large number of men and women who served during the First World War, the Second World War, and the ccof the names of these heroes.

World War I

Charlie Bounsall

Bert Latimer

Bert Edwards

Alf Edwards

Stan Dunn

Bruce Berry

Harold Van Deusen

Matthews

Gernsey McClellan

World War II

West Beach

Ben Servers

Andy Matthews

Ross Wright

Milt Corson

Marg Corson

Lew Burton

Bob Taft

Bill Currie

Norm Millen

Bill Servers

Paul Carmen

Ed Hicks

Bert Hutchinson

Bob McLeish

Richard Butler

Chuck Butler

Bob Fredericks

Lionel Parker

Jack Parker

Herb Goddard

Jack Rice

Bruce Lunney

Chester Jury

John Jury

Bill Street

Frank Edwards

Abe Bennyworth

Walter Bennyworth

Alton Hughes

Jake Mulholland

Jim Perris

George Young

Brian Fox Male

Dave Dobson

Jack McLaughlin

John Williams

Tom Woodlock

Art Dorney

Seth Hunt

Claire Jacobs

Roy Swindells

Larry Saunders

Bill Kilpatrick, Jr.

Earl Clark

Harry Chambers

Jim Thompson

Terry Dustin

Cove Road

Jack Carlton   John Foxe
Frank Piper   Howard Pickard
Chuck Ormsby   Roy Needs

East Beach

Billy Mitchell   Lorn McQuarrie
Chester Jenson   Bill Colville
Dr. Percy Ireland   Jack Night
Arnold Damant   Murray Bate
Jack Martyn   Leroy Short

Korean War

Gord Lawson
Chuck Butler

The Army of Occupation 1951

Andy Saunders

The Blue Ensign - The West Beach Standard

When Gary Cole was a boy, there was only one flag, and that was the Union Jack. Today we have many flags, every province, territory, city and many companies and organizations have their own flags. Unfortunately since 1965 Canada also has a new flag.

In this respect, West Beach also has its own flag; in fact, it had one before most other areas. The West Beach standard is the historic Blue Ensign, and it is a very colourful flag with a fascinating story and legend to tell. The Blue Ensign is first and foremost a naval flag and is, of course, naval blue in colour. It is the flag of the Royal Naval Reserve to the best of Gary Cole's knowledge. The West Beach standard displays the coat of arms of Canada on the fly and the Union Jack in the upper corner. How did the West Beach get this unique flag you may ask? Here is the story. In the early 1950s, the Beach Association decided to erect a flagpole on the sand spit that had formed in the harbour. This flagpole was a converted TV aerial anchored in cement with cross spars to fly storm warning flags. Mr. Bill Street (who was a school janitor in Toronto) gave the beach a woollen Union Jack, which flew from the main mast of the new flagpole. As a very young boy, Forest Dilling gave Gary Cole the honour of putting up the flag every morning and lowering it every night, as well as raising the storm flags when needed. This was a task which Gary Cole considered a great honour and one he performed proudly and faithfully for over 10 years.

In about 1955 Chief Petty Officer Alf Edwards RCN, who worked at the naval base in Toronto aboard HMCS York, gave the original Blue Ensign to the Beach. It was a wool bunting flag 6ft by 3ft in size and was flown from the flagpole for many years until it became known as the official flag of West Beach. A few years ago, Gary learned that a flag store in Barrie

Ontario still carried the Blue Ensign. These flags made of a less durable nylon material meant that they would only last for two summers before having to be replaced.

Gary now flies the Blue Ensign from his cottage, which is beside the boardwalk. Since most people are unfamiliar with this flag, he often receives questions about what it represents. Sometimes for fun, Gary will kid people by saying that it is the flag of the Royal Irish Navy. On one occasion when Gary jokingly told a beach visitor about the flag belonging to the Irish Navy, the fellow said: "okay, very nice, very lovely."

So that is the story of the famed Blue Ensign and how it came to West Beach and how, after 65 years, this unique and beautiful flag still waves over Port Darlington. The Old Ensign faded and tattered as it is, is still kept in a safe place and occasionally displayed on special occasions. The last time it was presented was at the 1998 West Beach Reunion.

The Chapel on the Hill

Like all respectable communities 70 years ago, Bowmanville West Beach had its own church. Mrs. Winfred Fox felt there was a need for a church, so she had one built on Cove Road. This church was an open-air affair with upright cedar posts and four foot high walls around the bottom; above these walls, it was open to the elements. The church had a four-sided cedar-shingled roof, and there was also a small bell tower in its centre. This bell was used to call the children to Sunday school and adults to church each Sunday. There was a pulpit and benches both inside and out where the parishioners could sit. The church was called "The Chapel on the Hill," and it claimed to be non-denominational, although it was common knowledge that the Cove Road cottagers, including the Fox clan, were predominately Baptists. Every Sunday, there were Sunday school classes for the children from 10:00 AM to 11:00 AM and each child was given a Sunday school newspaper that came from the Baptist Church in Toronto. Then from 11:15 till noon, church services for the adults were held.

Gary Cole, who was very attentive at Sunday school and who had learned and memorized all the "Beatitudes" (one each week), was the first child asked to get up in front of the congregation to recite them. Unfortunately, Gary got stage fright and was only able to remember one or two Beatitudes, much to the chagrin of the minister.

There was a man who came to Bowmanville by the name of the Reverend Joseph De Pencier Wright. He came from a very prominent Smith Falls and Barrett's Rapids Eastern Ontario family. Reverend Joseph De Pencier Wright was like a salesman for the church, and when a church fell on hard times, the reverend would arrive and attempt to motivate the local town's people to return to the church and build up the congregation. There was a small pump organ at the English Church in Bowmanville, and Reverend Wright convinced them to donate it to the Chapel on the Hill.

Reverend Wright christened four or five beach children at the Chapel on the Hill, and one of the Fox girls was married there. Anyone who was religious and lived on the beach could preach at the Chapel, they would only need to let the chapel committee know in advance, and they would be assigned a date on which they would give their sermon. The chapel committee would have little cards printed up with the date and times each person was going to preach, and they would send them out in June and again in August. Reverend Wright was the only known ordained minister to preach at the Chapel, and all others were lay preachers.

When Gary Cole first started going to the Chapel on the Hill, the first Sunday school teacher he remembers was Mrs. Carlton. The Carlton family was a very prominent family on Cove Beach, and were second in importance to the Fox family. Later a girl named Willa Simpson took over Sunday school teaching, and she also played the pump organ.

The Chapel on the Hill had initially been on the east side of Chapel Road (that runs north from Cove Road), but it later moved across the road. Over time the Chapel on the Hill congregation petered out, and it eventually closed as people had lost interest.

Chapel on the Hill

Chapel on the Hill

The Boathouses

In the 1920s and 30s, it was a widespread practise for young men on the beach to take their lady friends for leisurely rides up the river or for more romantic evening moonlit cruises on the lake in their rowboats or canoes. These activities led to the building of many boathouses in three different locations around Port Darlington Harbour.

- The first area was on Norton's Island, where there were four or five boathouses.
- The second was at the Honey Bridge, where another three or four boathouses stood.
- Thirdly, two or three stood near Mickey Kempthorn's just south of the CNR station west of Soper Creek.

Most of the names of the owners of these boathouses are now long-forgotten, but it is still pleasant to recall them as some have exciting stories to tell.

A bank robbery took place in Bowmanville in 1900. The thieves stashed some of the money bags in one of the boathouses at the Honey Bridge. The money bags were found by two small boys who returned it to the bank for a reward. Even so, the police never caught the thieves nor found the money.

The main concentration of boathouses was on the Harbor bank of East Beach, where there were about 20 of them. These well constructed East Beach boathouses seconded as sleeping cabins during the summer. The boathouses have changed hands many times over the years, and their owners formed a separate and unique community on the beach.

Although he has forgotten some, Gary Cole remembers many of the boathouse owners, but not all. They include:

Bruce Lunny	Phil Latimer
Jake Lunny	Murray Bate
Jim Thompson	Jack Martyn
Bill Kilpatrick	Bob Kent
Russ Brown	Barney Perry
Jack Knight	Frank Bottrol
John Osborne	Jim Garton
Lawson Kirkton	Arnold Deamont.
Bill Colville	

On West Beach, there were only three boathouses during Gary's lifetime. The first was built in the marsh behind Cylent Phore's cottage in the 1940s by Mr. Taylor, who kept a significant launch there. Mr. Taylor was a top executive at the Oshawa General Motors plant, and he had a cottage near the west-end of Crystal Beach. In the 1960s, this boathouse moved to the marsh area behind Mr. Taylor's cottage and was reached by a very long dock. Another boathouse was owned by Russ Hallman and located near where the Taylor boathouse first stood. It was initially owned by Roy "Red" Swindles, who had a cottage next door to the Grant Edwards cottage.

Gary Cole owned the last boathouse on West Beach, located near the Hallman's. Gary and his uncle Bill Currie built it when Gary was 16 years old. Later moved by Tom Wright and used as a small cottage on the lot formerly occupied by Sunny Side cottage. Tom then moved it to his cottage on Pigeon Lake in the Kawartha Lakes.

The Bill Colville mentioned here as owning the boat named Bonnie Gu-Brath and the Bill Colville mentioned in Zetta Riders Remembrances were two different people.

All of these Bowmanville Beach boathouses are now gone, and none remain.

Boat Houses Eastside Darlington Harbour

Bill Colville's Famous Launch

BONNIE
GU-BRATH
BOWMANVILLE

7

Karen Mulholland with East Beach Dancehall in the background

End of Summer Corn Roast on the Beach

The Lifeguards

Marion New (Professor New's daughter) was the first lifeguard entrusted with keeping the beach swimmers safe back in 1945-46. She was a volunteer lifeguard, and she also gave swimming lessons.

Around 1948 it was decided that a full-time lifeguard was needed and the Bowmanville Lions Club; a community service group took on the responsibility of finding and paying for a full-time lifeguard on the beach. Al Witherspoon was the first lifeguard that was hired. Al was a high school geography teacher, and he had been a captain in the Canadian Army, who commanded an artillery battery at Bedford Basin in Halifax, Nova Scotia. Besides his lifeguard duties, Al also gave swimming lessons to the beach children for three or four years. Al lived in Bowmanville, and he rode to the beach on his bicycle each day. He would go to Auntie Robinson's cottage and change into his swimming suit. Al would also take the temperature of the water every day with a glass thermometer and record the results in a book.

The next Lifeguard was Dorothy Ann Currie, who was the daughter of Bill and Ella Curie, and she lived on the beach. She got her training in Toronto, where she was part of a synchronized swimming group. She swam with Billy Mitchell from East Beach all around the lighthouse and back every evening. Dorothy Ann was undoubtedly the most popular of all the lifeguards, and on the days when the water was too cold to swim, she would take the children to the nearby park and do activities with them.

The next Lifeguard was a fellow named Bill Leper, who was from Toronto, and he worked as lifeguard for 3 or 4 years. Since Bill was not from Bowmanville, he boarded at the Dilling cottage, where he slept and ate his breakfast and supper. Bill was supplied with his lunch by a different cottage owner daily.

The next Lifeguard on the beach was a Hampton resident by the name of Art Yammer, who did the job for three or four years. Art owned a car that he drove to the beach each day, and he brought his lunch with him.

The next Lifeguard, who was also very popular, was a fellow named Larry Hancock, and he did the job for only one year.

David Millen was the next Lifeguard who also did activities with the children in the park and David was also very popular.

The next Lifeguard was Gail Mulholland, who is now Gail MacDonald. Gail stayed at Auntie Robinson's cottage, and was very popular with the beach children. Gail was the last of the lifeguards on the beach, although the park activities carried on for the children and one of the most popular teachers was Brad Brooks.

Over the years, the Lions Club was very generous to Bowmanville Beach by paying the Lifeguard's salaries and also supplying an excellent rowing dory boat for the Lifeguard to use in case it was needed to go further out into the lake and rescue a swimmer in distress. Gary Cole's father, Fred Cole, was very active in the Lions Club and was its president at one time. During the sports days on the beach, the lifeguards were responsible for running the water races.

After the Lifeguard Program ended, the Town of Bowmanville instituted another program called: "Summer Playgrounds for Kids". It was held at various parks around town including the West Beach park. Over the years several teenage leaders served at the beach, with Brad Brooks being the most popular of these. The program featured sports, crafts, and other activities all geared towards children ranging from six to fourteen years of age. The climax of each summer's schedule was the annual "Penny Fair" which featured a parade through the town led by the Legion Pipe Band culminating in a kid's carnival at the Lion's Center. Over the years, West Beach Park had a very prominent record for winning the first prize for floats in the parade. Several of these winners stood out and are long remember. One year Tom Wright and Crystal Beach's "Senator" Bob Taft built a gigantic birthday cake float complete with candles. Another excellent effort was the Mississippi riverboat the "Robert E Lee" complete with moving paddle wheels. Another year the parade's theme was "countries of the world" with West Beach representing Ireland. The float represented an "Irish Gypsy Tinkers Caravan" and pulled by Ralph Simpson's team of horses. Over 30 kids were dressed as leprechauns complete with large floppy Irish hats and shillelaghs; even the horses wore floppy Irish hats. Leading the West Beach contingent of the parade was Miss Robin Saunders with her flaming red hair and carrying the green Irish flag with its Golden Harp.

The parades, especially those won by West Beach produced great times and fond memories that will never be forgotten.

Gary Cole remembers an incident after the Legion Pipe Band had led one of the parades. A lady said to him, rather sarcastically: "the children shouldn't win any prizes as they didn't build the floats the adults did". Gary's non-sarcastic reply was: "hell we're all kids down there on the beach". The playground program which lasted many years was a wonderful program for all of Bowmanville especially the kids of the Town.

Fortunately, there was no drowning on the beach over the years, while the lifeguards were on duty.

Bill Leper & friends

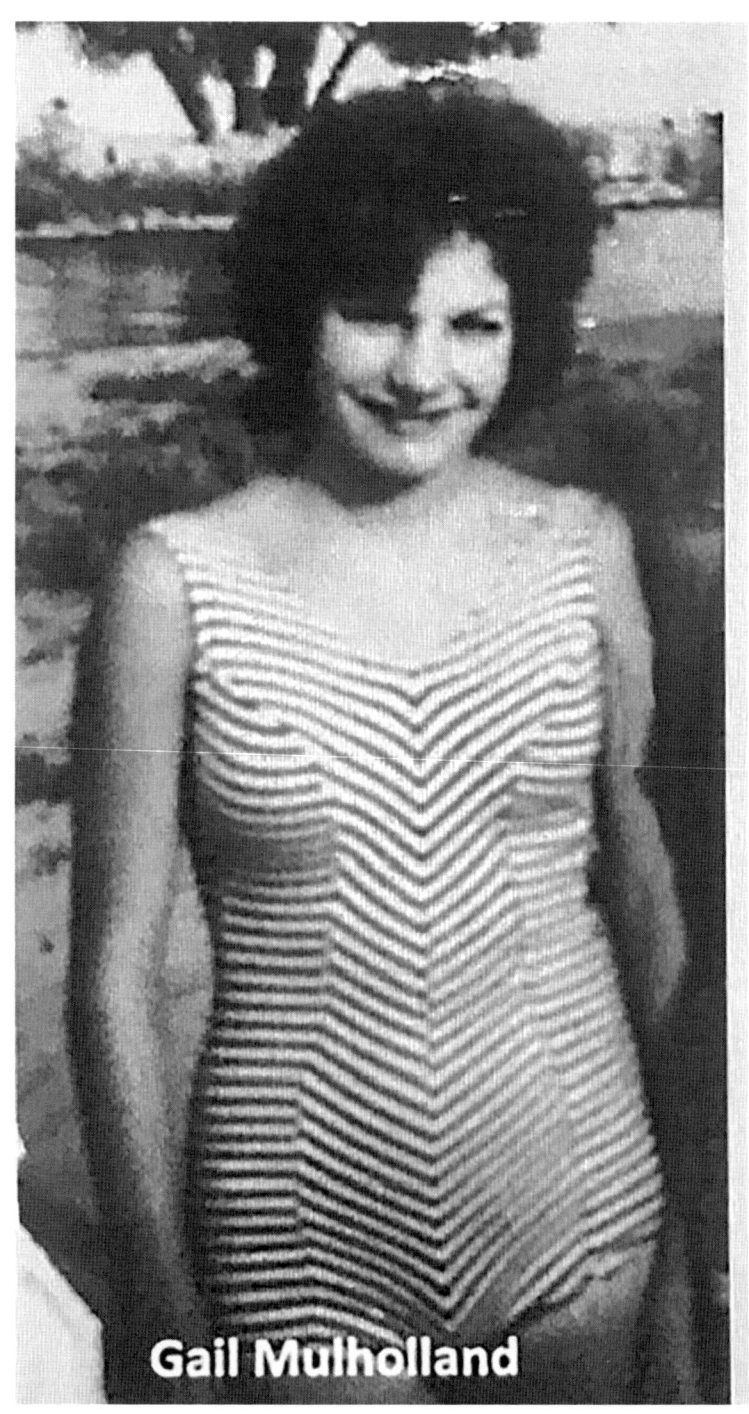

Gail Mulholland

Sea Cadet's Boat

Algae Problem on Bowmanville Beach

At one time in the 1950s and 1960s, there was a severe algae problem on Bowmanville Beach. Whenever a big storm came across Lake Ontario, it would rip the algae off of the bottom of the lake and wash it up on to the shore. When the algae appeared on the beach, it caused a big problem because of its odour and unpleasant appearance. It would start green, then turn black, then blue and finally white. The town government sent people down to Bowmanville Beach several times to rake up the algae and bury it under the sand but to no avail. There was just too much, and Gary Cole can remember seeing it extending 15 to 20 feet out from the shore in the water. It was so thick that little children could walk on top of it. Over time, the scientists found that the increased algae growth was caused by the use of phosphates in the dish and laundry detergent. These phosphates were getting into the lake water and acting as a fertilizer. As a result, the algae grew faster and soon grew out of control. Over the years phosphate was banned from detergents, and the algae problem went away for the most part. The problem was solved until the year 2000 when the algae started to come back again although not to the degree that it was back in the 1950s. Gary Cole sends a report yearly to the town government about the conditions on Bowmanville Beach, and four or five times he has mentioned that the algae is coming back.

Gary told the local municipal government that if the algae came back like before, they could kiss their park goodbye. Under those circumstances, nobody would go there to picnic or swim. The stink was so bad that it would be like having a picnic in a septic tank.

Gary urged the local municipal government to inform the Ontario government of the problem. It was suggested that they, in turn, should notify the New York State government which shares a coastline on Lake Ontario. Gary feels that somehow the phosphates are getting back into the lake water and causing the algae to start throwing again. We are lucky to have someone of Gary Cole's stature to be watching over our lake's coastline in Bowmanville. Gary is kind of like the canary in the coal mine, looking out for problems before they get out of control.

Unfortunately, Gary feels that the different levels of government are not paying enough attention to his warning about the resurging phosphate/algae problem.

Strawberry Fields Festival

On the weekend end of August 7, 8, 9 1970 there was a music festival similar to Woodstock held at Mosport Park north of Bowmanville. As a result, thousands of young people known as "hippies" converged on the Bowmanville area. For the most part, those who arrived were friendly, law-abiding young people and there was no violence, vandalism or mischief to speak of, although the illegal drugs and the public nudity laws went right out the window. At Tyrone Mill, Vanstone Mill, and Hampton Mill, many hippies swam in those ponds naked.

Most of the folks who came to the festival were from the United States although there were Canadians (some locals) among them. Because Mosport was such a hot and dusty place, word eventually spread that Bowmanville Beach was an excellent place to go for a skinny dip and so many hippies converged on that area also. One of the beach residences, George Steven, was annoyed with the amount of nudity and felt that the hippies should all be behind bars. But Doug Parker, a local Beach resident said, "You haven't got enough jails to hold them all." Fred Cole said: "they're just kids having fun and will be gone soon. After meeting one of the hippies, George had a change of heart and let some of the hippies sleep on his veranda. Forest Dilling, (who was the unofficial bird watcher of the beach), got a lot of use from his binoculars that weekend; later Forest's wife put an end to his bird- watching.

Some hippies erected a flagpole in front of the MacDonald's cottage, and put a brassiere and panties on it in place of the flag. By Tuesday, August 10th, 1970, all the hippies had left the beach. Rumours persisted that one fellow built a lean-to in the wooded area back of Mosport Park, where he lived for a couple of years. There were stories then and afterward that some hippies went missing and were never heard from again. These stories are a mystery, and one which survives to this day; whether they overdosed on drugs or were the victims of foul play, no one knows with certainty.

Doors Open

In June 2014, due to the efforts of our good friends: Faye Langmaid and Bernice Norton; four of our cottages on West Beach were privileged to be featured in the Clarington Doors Open event. The cottages that were open for public viewing were:

Jean Severs "Fernlighe,"
Shirley Fowler's "Irmadell,"
Gail & Chuck MacDonald's "The Dory Man"
Gary Cole's "Rathkeale."

During the Saturday event over 200 people attended and all seemed pleased and impressed. Most were amazed by the condition of the cottages, and many were surprised at their age, with one cottage dating back before the Great War (1914-18).

Also impressive was the fact that two of the cottages were in the hands of the granddaughters of the original builders. The West Beach community felt very proud and privileged to be part of this spectacular event because over the years Doors Open has featured some of the most stately and prominent homes in Bowmanville. The West Beach community wishes to thank Faye and Bernice for their efforts on behalf of the beach community.

Grand Reunion

In 1998 Ann Parker (nee Redman) the granddaughter of the Irmadells (Mr. and Mrs. Alf Fowler) came up with a great idea of holding a West Beach Reunion during the Civic Holiday. Ann Parker, Gail and Chuck McDonald, Mike Lootsma, Shirley Fowler, Peggy Mulholland, Sharon Eccles, Ron Parker, Brad Brooks, Steve Rider, and Gary Cole formed a committee. During the three- day event, several hundred former and present "Beachers" attended. They came from as far away as Summerland BC, Halifax Nova Scotia and Atlanta, Georgia. All the existing cottages were opened-up as Pavilions and featured: food, drinks & hospitality for the visitors. On Saturday a golf tournament was held followed by a big dance at the Bowmanville Legion Hall. On Sunday there was more fun including horseshoe matches followed by a corn roast which featured the biggest bonfire ever held on West Beach. On Monday for those still in attendance a massive roast beef dinner was held under the direction of Mike Lootsma, John Smith and John "Nick" Carter. All-in-all this was the most significant event ever held in West Beach in modern times. Credit goes to the organizing group and to those who helped in any way and to those who attended. Gary Cole is hopeful that the enjoyment of this reunion created lasting memories. Many reunion attendees had not been back to West Beach or seen each other in many years.

Barb Buttonshaw
&
Zetta Rider

The Reunion Committee

The Grand Reunion

Crystal Beach Cottages

While this is primarily a history of Bowmanville West Beach, it is first and foremost the story of the Port Darlington Harbor. West Beach is where Gary Cole lives and has been most involved.

However, as most people tend to think of Harbor Beach and Crystal Beach as the same, some mention of our sister beach, which is named Crystal Beach, should be made. Two unique Crystal Beach cottages are featured here. They are both in their way unique, with one being probably the first building erected on the beach and the other being the strangest ever constructed there.

The Log Cabin

Around 1948 Norm Green (who was married to Auntie Robinson's niece Dot White) bought the lakefront part of Daddy Couches' Camp Cozy lot and built a cottage there. Because of the wartime shortage of lumber, it was necessary to use six-inch diameter cedar logs. But unlike most log cabins, the logs in this cottage stood vertically. Norm was a carpenter by trade and did most of the work himself along with help from volunteers, friends and neighbours. Because of the wartime shortage, he had Joe Dilling pull and straighten nails from the salvaged lumber he had obtained for the floorboards and the roof joists. Cement was used to caulk the space between the logs. Since the logs were vertical Norm had trouble keeping the cement in place. The cottage had a front veranda, three bedrooms, a large living room with a fireplace, a kitchen and a bathroom. It was quite modern, even luxurious for the beach at that time.

Over the years the Greens rented the Log Cabin to several people including Mrs. Dorney, Mrs. Bill Street and for several years to George Young of Toronto and his family.

Later the Log Cabin was sold to Mr. and Mrs. Frank Hill who winterized it and added stucco. The cottage still stands but is now covered with vinyl siding and a bright red roof. It is unrecognizable as the log cabin that Norm Green built so many years before.

Lord Burton, The Marsh Toad
and the Three Grant Edwards

The oldest known building erected on West Beach and was initially built as a house although it eventually became a cottage. It was the only lath and plaster building on the beach. Its date of construction is unknown although it must have been very early. Gary Cole remembers seeing a circa 1900 picture of it, and it was ancient then. Its building site was at the south end of the old Frank Farm close to where the original Bowmanville Creek entered Lake Ontario. It was really on the surveyed end of Liberty Street. This fact caused some confusion in later years. The large Frank limestone farmhouse sits on Simpson Avenue where it curves to meet Baseline Road. Some old tales say that the Lord Burton house was Frank's first home. Although it was a long way from the central part of the farm, Lord Burton was one of the first people known to have lived in the house. He ran a small one-person fishing operation before 1900. Gary Cole's father often said that when he was a little boy around World War I, an elderly lady lived there. Her name was unknown, but everyone called her "The Marsh Toad." She had a garden near the marsh, where she grew a large amount of asparagus. Sometime in the early 1920s, the cottage had its most famous owner: Mr. Grant Edwards who owned an automobile dealership in Toronto. For our story, it is essential to note that there were, in fact, three Grant Edwards who lived on the beach over a 90 year period. Gary's father knew the first Grant Edwards, Gary knew the second Grant Edwards and as a boy, Gary also played with the third Grant Edwards.

The cottage had a large L-shaped open veranda facing the lake. A large living room, dining room/kitchen and upstairs there were four bedrooms. The east end became another bedroom after the screening of the veranda was done. The occupants only had squatters rights because the cottage was on the Liberty Street extension and the Town of Bowmanville owned the land.

Squatters rights could only be maintained if a Grant Edwards was living there. Over the years, this was always the case.

The first grant Edwards sponsored an excellent softball team which played in a league in the city of Toronto. On weekends during the summer Mr. Edwards often brought the ballplayers to his cottage, and on Sundays, they would play a team of West Beach boys on the sand in front of Camp Cozy. After the game the boys took the train back to Toronto. In Toronto, during the 1920s, baseball games were not allowed on Sundays.

One of the strangest events ever to happen on the West Beach centred on this cottage. In the late 1920s or early 1930s, a well- dressed man came to the beach and rented a room in the boarding house. He told everyone that he was a sanitation and health inspector for the city of Toronto and that he needed to inspect all the cottages on the beach. When he came to the Edwards cottage, he took one look at their canvas-covered, straw- filled mattresses and shook his head. He then ordered all of the beds be taken to the front of the cottage and burnt. Subsequently, this man was found to be an inmate who had escaped from an insane asylum. He was only posing as a sanitation and health inspector. Fortunately, he didn't say he was a building inspector, or he might have burnt the cottage down.

About 20 years ago, this cottage was sold by the 3rd Grant Edwards (Gary's childhood friend) to the Town of Bowmanville who had it torn down to make way for the parkette which is at at the far west end of the Back Road. It would be interesting to know if the spirits of some of the old Grant Edwards softball team players still hit the odd home-run there. They were outstanding ballplayers, and on most Sunday afternoons they had little trouble beating the boys of the West Beach pick-up team.

Zetta Rider's Remembrances

Here are the reminiscences of Zetta Latimer Rider who is a West Beach girl in every sense of the word.

"Mr. Stewart a West Beach resident who also ran the Sunday School in the Dancehall would regularly bring his Toronto Sunday school class down to Bowmanville Beach. One of his Sunday school students was my mother Dory Edwards. She was about 11 years old at the time and she fell in love with the beach and consequently convinced her mother, Annie Edwards, to rent a cottage there. My mother and a friend from Toronto would arrive on Sunday afternoons by train. Boyfriends from town would be waiting in there canoes at the Honey Bridge to paddle them down to the beach as there was no back road in those days. My mother first married at the age of 18, and when she would be at the beach and go to Joe Dilling's Dancehall, as a young widow she would take off your wedding ring."

The Latimers:

"William Clarke Latimer my grandfather owned three hotels one in Bowmanville (The Arlington which was beside the railroad tracks and the Honey Bridge), one in Port Perry, and one in Blackstock. One night in January 1904 my grandfather was going home in his buggy when he fell asleep. The horse knew his way home but on the way, workmen had taken out a bridge and the horse didn't notice. Subsequently, the workmen found my injured grandfather the next morning. As there was no hospital nearby he was put on a sleigh in Blackstock to be taken by train to Toronto, unfortunately, he died en route."

"My father Bert Latimer told me that when he and his brother were little and playing outside and if they became thirsty they would run into the Blackstock Hotel and get a small glass of beer to quench their thirst."

In September 1921 my mother Dory Edwards (along with my grandmother) went down to West Beach to recuperate from a broken arm. My father Bert Latimer was also recuperating from burning the candle at both ends in New York City where he was playing on stage on 42nd Street. At that time people had to go to the east side of the harbour and then cross the river by boat. My father was paddling his canoe along and offered my mother and grandmother a ride across the river which they refused. Although he did take their luggage across leaving them on the east side. My mother was furious but this didn't deter their romance as they got married in 1923."

"Long before my mother went to Bowmanville Beach it was known as Port Darlington. I think it was a big port back then and my father remembered going there on a ferry from Toronto."

How I met Bill Colville

"I was 10 years old and Bill was dating Dorell Byers from the East Beach. June Millen and I used to sit in the Dancehall to watch the big kids dance. Dorell and Bill were leading the line doing a dance called 'The Big Apple'. Bill took a shine to me and asked me to dance and I fell in love. Bill joined the Royal Canadian Air Force and he was stationed in BC. We would write back and forth and I would send him boxes and he would send me Christmas presents. I remember coming home from school one day and my mother said she had some bad news for me about Bill, I cried and cried."

William Freeborn Colville was one of three brothers from Bowmanville: Alex, Bill and John (AKA Sandy) all of whom were in the Royal Canadian Air Force and all of whom paid the supreme sacrifice during the war. Zetta subsequently married Len Rider and together they had three children: Stephen, Sidney, and Doug. There is more about the Latimer and Edwards families elsewhere in this book.

*It should be noted that the Bill Colville mentioned here and the Bill Colville mentioned else where in this book (who owned the boat named: "the Bonnie Gu-Brath) are two different people.

Arlington Hotel

Famous People of West Beach

Bowmanville Beach was a unique summer place, although it was difficult to access. Most of the land on which the cottages stood was leased and not owned by the cottagers. The Harbor Beach cottage land was owned by the Darlington Harbour Company and leased to the cottagers. The Crystal Beach land was owned by Mr. Possin and leased to the cottage owners there. Over time Mr. Possin sold the property to the Crystal Beach cottagers.

In the early days, practically anyone could afford to own a cottage on West Beach. For example, when Gary Cole's father bought their cottage in 1941, he paid $500.00 for it. The beach was a place for the ordinary people, the working people; there were very few professionals such as executives, doctors or lawyers etc.

There were also a lot of older people without a substantial means of support.

Even though the beach was an ordinary people's place, there were undoubtedly famous people who live there. By far, the most famous person and the richest was Roy Thompson. Mr. Thompson was a multi-millionaire tycoon in the newspaper business. He owned the Times of London newspaper, and he also held many television and radio stations. Mr. Thompson eventually acquired the title of Lord in England. When he was a kid, Roy's father was a barber in Toronto, and his mother's sister had married Frank Pethick, who was a barber in Bowmanville, and he had a cottage on the far end of Crystal Beach. Roy Thompson spent every summer at Bowmanville Beach with his aunt and uncle until Roy was 14 or 15 years old. Roy spent all of his boyhood summers at the beach and in an interview with the Toronto Star at one time, said that the happiest days of his life where the summers he had spent on Bowmanville Beach. Roy was a good man who donated to many charities, including the Thompson Hall in Toronto. During his youth, Roy Thompson was a radio salesperson, and one year, Roy went up to North Bay to try his luck at selling radios there. He didn't have much success because of the poor radio reception caused by the rocks in the area and because of the fact North Bay was so far away from any significant radio transmitter. Roy's uncle Mr. Pethick gave Roy $1000.00, which Roy used it to start a radio station in North Bay. Starting a radio station was how Roy Thompson got his start in the media business and also was the springboard to his later fortune. With a nearby radio station, Roy was able to sell many, many radios in the North Bay area. Roy never forgot Mr. Pethick's generosity, and he once told Gary Cole's father that he was doing okay because his nephew always looked after him.

When Sir John A Macdonald, the 1st Prime Minister of Canada, was having his last campaign in 1891, he went into Mr. Pethick's barbershop in Toronto for a shave. The Prime Minister had a rather large nose, and after Mr. Pethick had finished shaving one side of his face, he grabbed the prime minister's nose and turned him in the opposite direction. Sir John A Macdonald said, "Pethick, you are the only man who can lead the Prime Minister of Canada around by the nose." During that campaign, Sir John A Macdonald was giving out special medals, which bore his campaign slogan "The Old Party, The Old Flag, The Old Chieftain," and he gave one of these medals to Mr. Pethick. Years later, in 1957, when John Diefenbaker was elected prime minister, Mr. Pethick, who was the head of the Conservative Party in Bowmanville at one time, sent that medal to Mr. Diefenbaker who was quite a collector of Sir John A. Macdonald memorabilia. In Peter C Newman's book The Renegade in Power, which is the story of the Diefenbaker government, the incident of the medal and the Bowmanville barber (Mr. Frank Pethick) is mentioned.

Another famous person on the beach was Dr. Gordon Millen, a dentist who had a practice on Danforth Avenue in Toronto. He was also a member of the Toronto city council and an MPP for the Danforth Area. A ball field in the Riverdale Park Area called Millen Memorial Stadium was also named in his honour. One summer weekend, Dr. Millenn invited some of his Shriners friends to the beach, and they paraded around in their fez hats.

Dr. Millen's son-in-law was also a famous person on Bowmanville Beach; his name was Sid Smith; at one time, Sid became the captain of the Toronto

Maple Leafs and Sid played on a line with the legendary Teeder Kennedy. Sid was also the player-coach of the Whitby Dunlops when they won the World Hockey Championship in 1958.

Another famous person on the beach was Professor Chester W. New, who at one time ran for the Canadian Parliament as a Conservative candidate in Hamilton. More information about Professor New can be found in the description of his cottage Lakeside Villa elsewhere in this book.

Mr. Van Dusen, who owned a cottage on West Beach, also had his claim to fame. He invented and helped develop laughing gas, which dentists use during teeth extractions, and it was through this invention that Mr. Van Dusen made his fortune.

Another famous Bowmanville Beach Resident was Ted Bounsal, who was a professor of physics at the University of Windsor. Ted was also on the Windsor City Council, and an NDP MPP for the riding of Windsor Sandwich.

Another famous Bowmanville Beach resident was Trudy Young. Trudy, who was a renowned TV and movie actor. Trudy starred in the TV series Heidi and was also on the TV game show, Tic Tac Toe. Trudy also acted in the 1971 hockey movie Face-Off with Art Hindle.

PART TWO

E.E.E.E. "For Ease"

First owned by the Peck family this cottage was built in the typical West Beach design around 1920. The Pecks were related to the Stewarts who lived next door to the west. Mr. Stewart was a very religious man who held church and Sunday school services in his cottage and at the dancehall regularly.

In the late 1930s and 40s, E.E.E.E. was rented by Tommy Ross, who was the owner of the Royal Theater a cinema located in downtown Bowmanville at that time. Mr. Ross was a man of excellent character with a community-oriented personality who helped anyone he could. Tragically in 1947, Tommy died from smoke inhalation when he fell asleep while smoking a cigar at his home in downtown Bowmanville.

In the early 1940s, the cottage was bought by Fred Pethick a Toronto barber. Mr. Pethick had previously owned a cottage on Crystal Beach which was unfortunately destroyed by fire. There were unproven rumours that Mr. Pethick's cottage and his brother Frank's cottage next door, we're both victims of arson. The arson was rumoured to be the mischievous work of German prisoners- of-war from Camp 30. These prisoners were allowed on-their-honour not to attempt to escape and were allowed to roam freely about the town. Mr. Pethick named his Cottage E.E.E.E. which meant "For Ease." Fred Cole (Gary's father) helped carry a cement slab with E.E.E.E. embossed on it from the Pethick's old cottage site to his new cottage location. The cottage had been dark brown with green shutters and trim but Mr. Pethick had it painted white with green trim. After Mr. Pethick's death, ownership of the cottage went to his wife Rose and her daughter and son-in-law Mr. and Mrs. William "Bill" Currie, and their two daughters Joyce (Mrs. Harry Humble) and Dorothy Anne (Mrs. David Ault). Dorothy Anne was considered West Beach's most popular lifeguard.

Subsequent owner Mike Lootsma held E.E.E.E. for several years. Eventually, Port Darlington Harbor Company obtained the cottage and had it completely rebuilt. Next, the town of Bowmanville/Clarington obtained E.E.E.E. and once they had acquired they had it torn down, even though it was one of the best and most beautiful cottages on the beach.

Pethick Cottage

Restawhile

Prior to WWI Restawhile had initially been a two-story cabin which belonged to the Varco family. In the late 1920s Elgin Varco had it moved 30 feet closer to the lake. Over the next several summers, Mr. Varco had Bruce Lenny build several additions on to it. Elgin Varcoe was quite a character, and like many of the "Young Bucks" in the 1920s and 1930s, he owned a canoe of which he was very proud. At one point, Mr. Varco decided his son Michael should learn how to use a canoe properly. After several weeks of instruction, Mr. Varcoe decided Michael had become proficient enough with handling a canoe. He decided Mike should take all the kids on the beach for a ride up and down the lake in front of their cottage. Mr. Varco held a high position in the Bowmanville Goodyear Company, and he used to have his boss Mr. Cattran, (who ran the Goodyear plant) down to his cottage, for a few cocktails.

Once while the two men were sitting on the cottage veranda, watching Michael demonstrate his canoe skills, Michael accidentally clicked the gunwale with the paddle. Mr. Varco jumped up and told his son, "come here while I instruct you how to correctly paddle a canoe!" At the time Mr. Varco was wearing: white duck trousers, a white shirt, and a straw Panama hat. Mr. Varco got into the canoe, and since canoes are notoriously very tippy, Mr. Varco got in one side of the canoe and rolled out the other side into the water. He lost his glasses and Panama hat, which was found later by one of the beach children and, brought back to him. The kids on the beach, who were waiting their turn for a ride, saw the whole incident, but none dared to laugh. Later, when Mr. Varco came back to his front porch, his boss Mr. Cattran asked him, "what happened Varc was there a sudden cloudburst?"

After Mr. Varcoe passed away, the cottage moved to his daughter and son-in-law Nancy and Donnie Masters and their sons: John and David. Later on, Donnie took charge of the Goodyear plant in Collingwood. Later still he moved to the state of Georgia in the United States where he was made the president of the entire Goodyear Corporation.

Eventually, Mrs. Elgin Varcoe sold the cottage to Mrs. Rachel Stevens, who along with her son George, wife Kay, son Butch and daughters Wendy and Nancy enjoyed the cottage. George and Kay built a substantial addition onto the east side, changed the colour from yellow and green to dark brown with white trim and renamed the cottage "Moonfleet."

After the Stevens left the beach, Ted and Lynda Bonsall bought the cottage. Ted was a professor at Windsor University and a member of the Provincial Parliament. Ted, is a lifelong West Beach resident, who was raised at his family's cottage on Crystal Beach. Ted and his wife Lynda used the cottage for over 25 years, but in 2018 due to declining health, they were forced to relinquish their lease to the Town of Bowmanville. In February 2019 the town had Restawhile - Moonfleet (the oldest standing cottage on the beach) torn down.

Norjack

Norjack was owned from the 1920s, 30s, and 40s by Dr. Gordon Millen, (a one-time MPP from Toronto). Dr. Millen named his 20- foot long cedar-strip launch Norjack, after his two sons, Norman, and Jack. Dr. Millen was a dentist on Danforth Avenue in Toronto, and he was also an alderman in the city of Toronto. Dr. Millen was high up in the Shriners organization. On June 12, 1930, the Shriners held a convention in Toronto. The convention's location was in Canada because Canada still had legal alcohol while the United States was under prohibition at the time. Dr. Millen brought many of the Shriners for a day at his cottage at West Beach.

Toronto Mayor Ralph Day (who was an undertaker on the Danforth Avenue) was also there that day. The Shriners paraded around that day on the beach wearing their famous Fez hats. Dr. Millen had an outstanding 20-foot long cedar-strip launch which was used for waterskiing and surfing on the lake. Dr. Millen would surf behind his lunch and end-up right on the beach. He would do a cartwheel from his surfboard right in front of his cottage.

Unfortunately, Dr. Millen passed away at a young age. Dr. Millen's brother-in-law Mr. Hunter and his wife would come every spring and open up Norjack for the Millens, They would clean, and painted, etc. Mr. Hunter was an ordinary type of guy who sold draft beer in the local beer parlour. After the Hunters finished their work, they would always leave before the Millens arrival. Jack Millen, Gordon's son, was also a dentist; in fact, he took over his father's practice after he died at a young age.

Gordon's daughter June was married to Sid Smith the captain of the Toronto Maple Leafs from 1955 to 1956, and they visited the cottage quite often. Sid played on a line with the famous Maple Leafs captain Teeder Kennedy. After Sid Smith retired from the Toronto Maple Leafs, he went on to become the playing coach of the Whitby Dunlops. The Dunlops won the 1958 World

Ice Hockey Championships in Russia. Sid also worked for the Dunlop Rubber Company in Whitby. Sid also worked for the Labatt's brewery as a goodwill ambassador to supplement his hockey player salary. Sid's son Blaine was once asked whether his dad ever received a signing bonus with the Toronto Maple Leafs.

Blaine said: "yes one time Con Smyth gave my dad a Toronto Maple Leafs windbreaker and ten dollars." Down on the Bowmanville West Beach Sid just wanted to be known as one of the guys he didn't want any special recognition or treatment. Sid also played a lot of softball on the beach. One of Gay Cole's old friends, Clint Ferguson, who often played with Sid on the same team, said: "Sid was always just one of the guys and a real gentleman."

Sid Smith needed a knee operation, and after the surgery, he caught a virus and passed away. After this unfortunate incident, Sid's son called Gary Cole and asked him if it would be okay to sprinkle Sid's ashes along the beach. Gary said: "yes, of course, no problem." Sid's son recalls that of all the places that his dad had visited and all the people that he met during his career, his memories of Bowmanville Beach were his fondest. So with his ashes sprinkled on the beach he is still there, the place he loved the most.

Moonshine

One of the oldest buildings on the beach; this two-story cottage was built in 1904 by Roger Fishleigh, with scrap lumber from the old South Ward Tabernacle. Also made from the South Ward Tabernacle's lumber was Gus Bounsall's Cottage on Crystal Beach, later owned by Senator Bob Taft. Bob Taft got his nickname "Senator" because he had the gift of gab, and was a good talker.

The Southward Tabernacle was torn down in 1904, and the scrap lumber from it was reused to build cottages on West Beach. The location of the Southward Tabernacle was on the corner of Ontario Street and Liberty Street, where the self-serve gas station now stands. It was a non-denominational church, as anyone could go there on Sundays for the service. There wasn't a full-time minister, so usually; a lay preacher gave the sermon.

Moonshine was one of two cottages that were known by this name (the other being: "Leaside") and occupied by an elderly lady named Mrs. Mathers. With no disrespect, a young Gary Cole (along with the other beach children) considered Mrs. Mathers to be a witch when he delivered her newspapers back in the 1940s. In reality, she was a nice person. The children on the beach also thought the cottage haunted. The rear of the cottage had a knothole in the siding. On the inside of the cottage, someone placed a mirror over the knothole. When the children looked into the knothole to see inside all they could see was their own eyeball. For this reason, the children thought that the cottage haunted and its owner was a witch.

Later the cottage was owned by the Downey family and for several years it was also occupied by Robert Stinner of Toronto.

Moonshine was always painted yellow, although it was painted dark brown by its last owners Jack and Madeline Parker. Jack Parker had been a plumber in his father's business in Bowmanville and later moved to Ajax where he started his own plumbing business. The Parker family were very musical, and the children played the guitar and other instruments as well. On weekends Mrs. Parker, who played the ukulele, would have a musical get together with many people singing and playing instruments. David Parker, who was a son of Mr. and Mrs. Parker was Gary Cole's best friend as a child. Jack and Madeline Parker named their other son Ronnie. While both Parkers were very good on the guitar, Ron was exceptional, and he had an excellent singing voice. He entertained at many bonfires and other Beach functions.

At the end of WWII, some people started living in their West Beach cottages year-round, Moonshine was one of these.

Mr. Stinner, who also lived in the cottage, had a car with no hood, and when it would start to rain, he would go out and drape a raincoat over top of the engine. Unfortunately, Moonshine was torn down in 1970.

Eldorado - Doryman

This large modified West Beach style cottage was built for Miss Edith Robinson by Bowmanville carpenter Charlie Heal who was the premier carpenter in Bowmanville back in the 1920s and 1930s. It later belonged to the Van Dusen family and afterwards sat empty for many years.

Auntie Robinson owned three different cottages on the beach during different times. She also held a boarding house in Toronto where she was the cook and as well as the housekeeper. She enjoyed taking care of people, and one such person who received her loving care was Peggy Kelly. Peggy Kelly's father asked Auntie Robinson to look after his daughter, and over time Auntie Robinson became a surrogate mother to Peggy.

Mr. Van Deusen, who owned the cottage at one time was a Toronto dentist who had a connection to the early invention of nitric oxide (AKA laughing gas). Mr. Van Deusen's children were Helen Van Deusen (a victim of polio) and Harold who served in the Canadian military during WWI. Auntie Robinson was also a practical nurse, and she gave care to Helen Van Dusen. The Van Deusen's who were from Toronto, sold their house there and moved to Bowmanville. They bought a house on the corner of Horsey Street and Elgin Street across the road from the present- day Marnwood Nursing Home. At the time their home was the only one in Bowmanville with an elevator. They used the elevator so their daughter Helen could travel between the floors of the house. The Van Deusen's owned two seldom-used cottages on the beach, one beside the other.

The cottage was finally bought for a nominal sum by Jim Thompson and later sold to Mr. John Moore of Toronto. Mr. Moore made extensive renovations, and in 1996 he sold it to long-time beach residents: Gail and Chuck McDonald, who also made many improvements. Since Gail had a close connection with Miss Edith "Auntie" Robinson (who became a surrogate grandmother to her), to her the cottage was like coming home. The McDonald's have renamed the cottage "The Doryman" about Chuck's Cape Breton Island heritage. Traditionally the cottage was yellow with green trim, but John Moore painted it robin's egg blue. The McDonald's have since painted it more of a dark green colour with yellow trim.

Eldorado Cottage

Beach Girls 1930's Macdonald Cottage behind

Robber's Roost - Adam's Apple

This small cottage was built in the West Beach style by Harold Van Deusen for his sister Helen in the 1920s. The cottage sat vacant for many years and was rented over the years by Jack Parker, Bob Kent, and Len Hooey. The cottage initially was not named, however during Jack Parker's tenancy; it was called "The Robbers Roost."

It was next bought for a small sum by Jim Thompson after having had several short-term owners. Later it was bought by John Moore, who did many renovations to the cottage. After John Moore, it again had several different tenants, including "Dutch" who was known mysteriously as the beach habitant who came, left and then never returned. The next owner was a man by the name of Bill Cullen. He sold the cottage to a German fellow who was an caretaker at St. Mary's of the Pines Church in Scarborough. Because of his Deutsch accent, he got the nickname, "Dutch." After he bought the cottage, Dutch came down one spring weekend to open up the cottage, and while he was there, he had a few beers with some of the local fellows on the beach including, Gary Cole. During that weekend Dutch told the people gathered that he had to leave but that he would be back the following weekend and he'd supply the beer, but he was never heard from again. The rumours at the time were that Dutch had bought the cottage to help recuperate his ailing wife but that her illness had worsened and she suddenly passed away.

Heartbroken, and because the cottage reminded him of his wife, Dutch never had the heart to come back to Bowmanville Beach again.

The cottage sat empty for many years until it was sold to Donna and Don Adams by Dutch in 1995. The painting scheme on this cottage initially being yellow with green trim but Don Adams had it painted gray with blue-gray and burgundy trim, these days the cottage is white with dark blue trim. Donna has sadly passed away, but Don, (who now lives in Wilmot Creek) and his son still have and use the cottage.

The Boarding House #2 Rathkeale

This large cottage was part of Mr. Berry's boarding house complex, but unlike the Brook's cottage it was used exclusively to house male borders although the male borders took their meals in the main Boarding House #1. Downstairs there were two open verandas and a living room while upstairs there were four bedrooms and an open veranda. Sometime later, Mr. Berry screened in the porches and added a kitchen/dining room, and he rented it out to families.

Charlie and Irene Severs who owned the cottage later, enclosed the open western veranda and made it into a storage shed. The Severs subsequently sold the building to Steve Babich. The next owners were Paul Carmen and his family, who sometimes rented the cottage to other people. Mr. Carmen was not impressed when he discovered that one of his tenants had painted the building a lime green colour instead of white with green trim.

In 1985 the cottage was bought by Mrs. Edith Cole, Gary's mother, and it was named: "Rathkeale" after Gary's grandmother's home village in County Limerick Ireland. In recent years Rathkeale has undergone extensive renovations, including new board and batten siding over the original clapboard. Although it is now nearly a hundred years old, Rathkeale is still considered one of the foremost cottages on West Beach. In the last few years, Gary has put a metal roof on the cottage as well as the storage shed and laid-down laminate tiles on the interior floors. This cottage is almost two stories high, making it the largest on the beach and is the only cottage with a separate dining room.

Mr. Berry's Boarding House

Lake Side Villa

This cottage was the first ever built on West Beach. It was the only cottage that rivalled the swanky cottages on the upper East Beach. It was built in 1890 by Dr. H.L. Reid who named it Lakeside Villa.

Dr. Reid was a doctor in Bowmanville and also a member of the Port Darlington Harbour Company's board of directors it's believed this is why he got to build his cottage there.

The clapboard cottage was painted dark yellow with dark green trim and had a cottage roof on the center part. However, Gary Cole has a picture taken before 1900, showing it with a gable roof but the reason for the alteration is unknown.

In 1900 Dr. Reid sold the cottage to well-known Bowmanville drugstore owner John H.H. (Hains Hezekiah) Jury. Mr. Jury was a native of Port Perry, but he took his apprenticeship to be a pharmacist in Bowmanville. Later he became a partner in the pharmacy and then he was the owner. Eventually, Mr. Jury had a chain of drugstores: one in Bowmanville, one in Oshawa, and one in Whitby. Later, Mr. Jury teamed up with Mr. Lovell from Oshawa to form the Jury and Lovell drug stores. Mr. Jury was an entrepreneur, who was ahead of his time. He had a lot of patent medicines that he sold in his drug stores. One of these claimed to be a cancer cure. He also sold necklaces (which Gary Cole's grandmother Mrs. Severs made) that if they were placed around a child's neck would make the child's teeth grow in straight. Mr. Jury also exported these necklaces to Germany. Mr. Jury's house in Bowmanville became the Bowmanville Museum on Silver Street in 1961. Around 1929 Mr. Jury built the Jury Jubilee building on King Street West at Silver Street in Bowmanville, where the Cole Barbershop eventually stood. With its Italian villa-style, it was considered one of the most classical buildings built in

Bowmanville. At the time of the Great Depression, Mr. Jury was considered a millionaire. Mr. Jury had two children named Gordon and Mildred.

Lake Side Villa is on the corner of the Beach and the harbour, next to the sand fence. The Port Darlington Harbor Company erected the sand fence to keep the continuing blowing sand from silting up the harbour. This fence lasted well into the 1920s. Gary Cole recalls seeing the original stump ends of the posts in the 1950s. Originally the harbour company had a man with a horse and scoop who leveled the sand on the beach each summer.

When the Harbor company business began to decline after World War I, they no longer maintained the fence. It eventually collapsed, and sand began to fill up the harbour.

Lakeside Villa was used for many years by Mr. Jury's daughter Mildred, her husband Dr. Chester New and their three children: Gordon, Margaret and Marion. Mr. New was a professor of Ancient history at McMaster University in Hamilton. He also wrote history textbooks for Ontario schools, grades 11 and 12. Mr. New had extensive knowledge of ancient and modern history. Mr. New did not socialize much with the other people on the Beach and Mrs. New was a painter and two of her oil paintings: one is of the marsh, and the other is a panorama of the cottages on West Beach. They are both in the Bowmanville Museum at 37 Silver Street, where they are hanging in Mildred's bedroom. Mrs. News daughter Marion was the first lifeguard on the Beach. Mr. New suffered from severe arthritis, and he quite often had to be helped up to his bedroom on the second floor. There was a spare bedroom on the main floor, which he could have used but didn't, for unknown reasons. The cottage was quite large, by West Beach standards. It was the only full two-story building erected on the Beach. On the ground floor there was: a deep veranda, a large living room, a kitchen and a seldom-used back kitchen which was full of odds and ends. Upstairs there were: four small bedrooms and one large bedroom on the western end of the cottage. On the eastern side overlooking the bathhouse, there was a five-foot by four-foot balcony which was used by the News for their morning toilet where they brushed their teeth. In the spring and the fall, when the News opened and closed the cottage, Gary Cole would get Miss Robinson's wheelbarrow and move the entire luggage etc. to and from their cottage. Ten trips were needed to move everything.

Mr. New would give Gary 25 cents for doing the work. The News would also bring their small refrigerator from the Jury home at 37 Silver Street to the Beach via taxi. Once Gary got Don Green to help move the News stuff, but Mr. New wasn't too happy about it because now he had to give them both 25 cents. Years later, when the News was getting older, they had to leave the Beach. On the last day, Mr. New gave Gary $10.00. On one occasion, about a month after the News left the Beach for the last time, a man came into the Cole barbershop asking the whereabouts of Mr. Chester New. This fellow had come on his mission from London, England. Gary told the man that Mr. New had left the Beach and gone back to his home in Hamilton, Ontario. Gary gave the man Mr. News address and telephone number but heard nothing more about it. Although about a week later, the word reached Bowmanville that Mr. New had passed away.

While it started as the fanciest cottage on West Beach, Lakeside Villa was like a time capsule. Nothing ever changed, not even the furniture. In Gary Cole's capacity as professor News chore boy in the 1950s, he used to marvel at the various antiques the cottage held. Of particular interest were the beds. The News slept in the first two bedrooms where they had modern beds. The other bedrooms had beds with a 2" x 4" wooden frame and legs. Instead of springs, these beds had criss-cross hemp ropes, these ropes were tightened with knobs, like the strings of a violin. For mattresses, there were canvas bags filled with straw. The bedrooms were small, approximately 5 feet by 8 feet with only: a single bed, and a small table with a washbasin. In the living room, there was a large table about 10 feet long and 4 feet wide. In the back kitchen was the biggest icebox Gary Cole has ever seen. He surmised that it must have come out of a butcher shop. Beside the cottage next to the harbour and close to the lake was a cabin used as a bathhouse. This cabin was approximately 12 feet by 6 feet and used by the News as a place to change into their bathing suits. Dividing the bathhouse meant the west half could be used as an outhouse and the east half used for storage.

One year Gordon New entered the annual horseshoe contest. He partnered along with Burt Hutchinson, and they won the contest that year. The prize was two beer glasses which would have been of no use at all to the News. Mr. News used to get a lot of important mail and manuscripts delivered to him at the beach post office from the museum in London, England. Gary Cole was the postman on the West Beach, and he carried these letters and documents to Mr. New. Mr. and Mrs. New loved each other very much and were devoted to each other. In the summertime in the evening, they would sit on their front porch and take turns reading from their history books aloud to each other. The children on the beach would often hide in the poplar bushes close by and listen.

The spring opening of Lake Side Villa was, of course, quite an event and several funny things happened over the years. Before the News arrival, Auntie Robinson would spring clean the cottage. Jake Mulholland would do the heavy work of opening the shutters. Gary Cole was the News luggage boy, and each year he waited for their arrival. One year Auntie Robinson decided that a pair of curtains needed washing. Like everything else in the News cottage, these curtains were ancient. After washing the curtains in Auntie Robinson's washing machine, they disintegrated into fragments. Another year the News decided that the old place needed a coat of paint.

Because the cottage was so large, Jake recruited the help of Bert Hutchison. The News, who were older at the time and rather frugal, were not in touch with the wages of the day. When Jake and Bert finished, their pay was about $3.25 just enough to buy a case of beer. They bought a case and drank it on the back kitchen roof. If he had known, the professor would not have been impressed.

Another time Miss Auntie Robinson (a prim and proper lady, but who also had an excellent sense of humour) observed that "Professor New, knows what King Tut had for breakfast but can't remember what he had for his breakfast." It was true; Mr. New was the prototype of the absent-minded professor.

Another strange thing that happened there was when several young girls from the area of the beach (who will remain nameless but they know who they are) decided to scare the News by shining a flashlight in the windows at night. The girls were lucky that Auntie Robinson did not find out about their escapades. After the News death, Paul Shulga and family used the cottage, for a few years. In the spring of 1967, Lakeside villa mysteriously burnt to the ground, the only serious fire in the history of the West Beach.

Jury & New family on beach

Cliffview - The Hutch

Cliff View cottage was for many years the summer home of Mrs. Beatrice Bakewell and her daughter Lorna, her husband, Bert Hutchison and their daughters Judy and Sharon. This cottage received its name Cliff View because at the time it was built (1936), the cliffs to the east were visible. However, over time sand buildup obscured the cliffs and making them no longer viewable. Subsequently, the cottage was renamed "The Hutch" after the Hutchison owners.

Claire Bakewell and his son Bruce built this cottage. Initially covered with yellow clapboard siding, Mrs. Bakewell changed the siding to brown insul-brick in 1944. Made with a cottage style roof, Cliff View had a stone fireplace, and metal roof added in 2018.

Cliff View is one of the most modern and well-maintained cottages on the beach. Cliff View is used today by Sharon and her family including grandson Tristan, a 5th generation Cliff View resident.

Mr. Hutchison worked for McLean - Hunter, a communications business in Toronto. Weekend invitations were extended by Mr. Hutchison to his co-workers twice a year. Once in the spring and again in the fall. Mr. Hutchison's daughters Judy and Sharon (who lives in Bala Ontario) now own the cottage. Judy's husband's name is Alex Ginou. Sharon spends all her summers at West Beach. Sharon's husband Ross Smith and son Corey also spend time at the cottage. Ross and Corey run the annual Horseshoe Tournament every year which usually draws a crowd of about a hundred people. Gary Coles says: "Mr. Hutchinson was a quality guy, it was a great pleasure to know him and call him a friend."

Aunties

Strangely enough, this white cottage, which overlooks the harbour, to the best of Gary Cole's knowledge, never had an official name. It was commonly known as "Auntie's" after its owner. It was built about 1932 by Charlie Heal and was the third of three cottages owned by Miss Edith "Auntie" Robinson. Made with a cottage style roof, it had a large veranda, three bedrooms; a large living room (with a red fireplace) and a huge kitchen. During Miss Robinson's time of ownership, the cottage was a haven for all of West Beach's children. These youngsters helped Auntie Robinson with various chores, and they always enjoyed her storytelling abilities and positive encouragement. Often Auntie would have the children in for the evening for roasted marshmallows while she played her Alto harp. Every fall the kids would pick elderberries, which Auntie would then make into jam.

She would give each child a jar in the spring to be refilled again in the fall. Gary Cole can still envision those small jars topped with paraffin wax and recall the excellent tasting jam inside. One time Auntie had the children collect driftwood from the riverbank and the front Beach and pile it beside her cottage for firewood. She had Gary, her nephew Don Green and Bruce Durno cut the wood up with her cross cut saw. As a reward, she offered to make all the pancakes that the boys could eat. Gary and Don both ate four pancakes each while Bruce, who had an intellectual disability (but healthy as a horse) ate 12-15 pancakes himself. Auntie said; "that's enough, off you go home." Auntie was one of the first cottage owners on the Beach, and she lived there her entire life. One of Auntie's stories tells about someone catching several Pike in the marsh. They invited the whole Beach, (at that time ten people) to a fish supper at Sandhurst, the Rice family cottage.

The dinner was held on an unscreened porch, when the first fish were carried in it covered in flies. When Auntie saw this, she made a polite but firm excuse and left without eating anything.

After Auntie's time, the cottage belonged to her niece, Peggy Mulholland and family. Peggy's family included daughters: Gail and Karen and son Howard as well as grandchildren: Brent, Kelly and Cassie.

Auntie Robinson was the matriarch of the Beach as she was well respected and loved by one and all. For many years Auntie's cottage was a focal point for fun and social activities on the Beach. When she eventually left the Beach, a lot of the old West Beach went with her.

Seymour Cottage

The cottage named Seymour was built for Dean Hodson and his family around 1938 by a Bowmanville carpenter named Les Brooks. Mr. Brooks built this cottage in about a week, he started construction on a Monday, and the Hodsons moved in on the following Friday or Saturday night.

This small cottage was built with a West Beach cottage roof and had additions added to the front and back. For unknown reasons, Mrs. Hodson didn't like the cottage, and as a result, the Hodsons only stayed there for a short period-of-time. Mr. Hudson owned the White Rose gasoline station on the corner of King and Liberty Street, where he had a snack bar, which was very popular selling hot dogs and ice cream, and upstairs above the garage, there was a dancehall. Mr. and Mrs. Hodson owned a house in town that is now known as the Bethesda house, which is located on the south side of Queen Street to the east of Rotary Park.

"Seymour" was later owned as a summer home by Mrs. Winnie Wonacott and her three daughters: Connie, Dot and Joan. Mrs. Wonacott painted it white with light blue trim and added a brick fireplace, and she later sold it to her brother, Tommy Woodlock.

Later owners were Peggy and Norman "Jake" Mulholland, Abraham Hilts and Seymour English. It is now owned by Dave "Tire man" since Dave's last name is not known and as he worked in Ajax where he sold automobile tires, he became known as: "Dave the Tire man."

The cottage was named "Seymour" because Seymour English loved to look out at the lake and "see more" water. Mr. English came from Markham Ontario, and he also worked at the Bowmanville Boy's Training School north of town.

Willow Nook

This cottage has one of the strangest stories to tell of all the cottages on West Beach. It was kind of a makeshift affair with a curved roof and was built originally as Loll Majaus's houseboat. In the summer, its location was in the Marsh near the ferry dock. In the winter, its location was on Norton's Island, just south of Highway 401 and east of Liberty Street. Sometime around the WWI, Bill "Pop" Quinn bought it and moved it to his harbour front lot. Pop Quinn added a veranda, a back kitchen and one of its unique features was a central skylight. Bill Quinn had lost one of his arms in an industrial accident while working for a rubber company in Toronto where his arm had got caught in a belt or a press. Bill Quinn's disability meant employment opportunities were in short supply, and he was one of the few men that were almost always present on the beach. Bill's job was to repair the beach's boardwalk that ran all along the beach at the time. Those boardwalks were similar to the ones that were put in the trenches in Europe during WWI. They were made of two by fours with boards nailed across them. At that time, the cottagers paid a beach fee of $10 per year to maintain the boardwalks, collect the garbage and removal of the night waste. Since Bill Quinn was responsible for this work, he was exempt from paying the beach fees. Bill also had an artificial arm that he rarely wore except when he would take his boat out on the lake. He found it easier to row the boat with two hands instead of one. His boat was not technically a rowboat, but a rowing boat. It had the shape of a 16- foot long canoe with a point at both ends. Two men would row it with a third man controlling the rudder and steering the boat at the stern.

Norton's island, when it still existed, measured approximately 40 ft by 20 ft and located east of where animal control building is today. It was in the middle of the nearby creek, which flowed on both sides of the island. During the 1950s, with the construction of Highway 401 through Bowmanville, the creek was diverted so that it only flowed on one side of Norton's Island. There were five or six boat houses on Norton's Island at the time. In those days, few people had cars, so people from town would ride their bicycles to Norton's Island and park them there. They would then use their rowboats and row down to their cottages on the beach.

Later owners were John Williams, Jack & Hazel McLaughlin and Stan & Linda Brown. Willow Nook was initially painted lime green, and the Williams family changed its colour to pink. The McLaughlin family added gray insul-brick siding and named it Willow Nook, and had it demolished in 1998

The Bruce Berry Cottage

At one time, people had to travel across the railway tracks near Liberty Street to reach West Beach. The crossing was unauthorized, so there were no flashing lights that warned people of approaching trains. The Beach Association stationed a man at the railway crossing with a flag and a lantern. He warned approaching cars that a train was approaching. They also supplied a hut for the crossing guards to sit in and take refuge from inclement weather. The shed was eventually moved to the harbourfront by Tommy Ross, and he sold it to Bruce Berry around 1939.

While Bruce added several additions over the years, he never gave the cottage a name. Bruce was a WWI veteran, and his wife Leona was the daughter of Billy "Pop" Quinn. Bruce first worked for a big car dealership in Toronto, and he later worked for Cliff Mills in Oshawa, where he became a parts manager. While Bruce never had any children, he was always kind to all the kids on the beach. Gary Cole remembers well seeing a large artillery shell, which Bruce used as a door-stop in his cottage. A strange event occurred one winter in the 1940s when Bruce and his wife drove down to their cottage one Sunday morning from Toronto. They parked their car on the East Beach and walked across the ice to the west side. They spent the afternoon sitting on their sofa enjoying sandwiches, a thermos of coffee and several cigarettes. When they returned in the spring, all that remained of their couch were the springs and the wooden frame. One of their cigarette butts had caused the sofa's upholstery to smoulder away without actually bursting into flame. It was a close call for the cottage and the rest of the beach also.

Around 1957 Bruce sold the cottage to Gord Greer of Oshawa and his wife Jean (an attractive red-haired gal). Later the cottage owners were the Hatfield family, who added some new siding.

Other owners were a brother and sister whose names were: Morgan and McCrimmon. There were four adults and six kids, and since the cottage was small, it was very crowded.

The last owners were Max Blackburn who was known as "The Blind Man" and his partner Edith Procno. Max was a large man who was an excellent pianist, even though he was stone blind.

Cheerio

This cottage built on the harbour front around 1910 was one of the oldest on the beach. It was, in fact, the first beach residence of the Fox family of Cove Road; who rented it for one summer before WWI. Although it's doubtful, they would like it known that they were once, "River Rats."

For many years this cottage belonged to Mrs. Eleanor Durno, a Toronto Telegram newspaper employee. She named the cottage "Cheerio" after a wartime entertainment group which she organized and ran. During her time, the cottage was painted white with royal blue trim and was always full of happy young people.

During Mrs. Durno's time, Cherrio was a continual hub of activity and entertainment. Her group Cherrio provided most of the entertainment for the concert on Civic Holiday. During the Second World War, Mrs. Durno's group entertained soldiers and raised money at War Bond drives. During those days, both the Telegram and the Toronto Star newspapers were involved in supporting the war effort. Mrs. Durno had three sons: Bill, Mac and Bruce. Bill and Mac along with Patty Welsh and Glen Virtue played the guitar and sang in the group before they joined the army. Back when Mrs. Durno's group performed, were wonderful times for the folks on the beach.

The cottage was sold after Mrs. Durno's death, to Miss Nina Creamer, a beautiful Italian/Canadian singer who was in the Cheerio Group.

Later, when the beach was looking for someone to cook for the Hawaiian Luaus, Gary Cole approached Seth "Snuffy" Hunt and asked him to take on the job which he agreed to do. There would be 50 to 60 people at those events. It was during one of these Luaus that "Snuffy" met Nina Creamer and within a year they were married. "Snuffy" Hunt came from Pennsylvania, and he had been a cook in the United States Navy. After the war, he travelled to

Canada and married a girl from Bowmanville named Helen Woods. Seth opened an auto body repair shop which he called: "Snuffy's." It was after his first marriage ended that "Snuffy" came to the beach and met Nina Creamer. In later years they lived at Wilmot Creek, and Snuffy was very active in the Bowmanville Legion, where also he did a lot of cooking.

Davelie

Davelie had initially been only a small cabin, which was built by Miss Edith Robinson. It was the first of three cottages she would eventually own on the beach. Miss Robinson occupied Davelie for several years along with her two nieces and a nephew. The niece and nephew's last name was White, and their mother was Mrs. Robinson's sister. Marnie White married Bruce Murchison, who was also a Bowmanville Beach resident. Another sister: Dorothy White married a fellow named Norman Green who also built a cottage on West Beach. Miss Robinson also had a nephew named Don White, and the Whites would come and spend most of their summers there.

Eventually, Mrs. Robinson decided to sell Davelie cottage to a family named: Simpson and move to another West Beach cottage named: "The Dory Man." Gary Cole remembers very little about the Simpsons except that they must have been Scottish because they named their daughter Ismay.

Over the years several additions were added to Davelie to give it a rather unique and strange appearance, even for the West Beach. In the late 1930s, it was bought by Dave Ault, a Brading Brewery salesman, who named it after his children Shirley and Velma and David. Mr. Ault was an avid fisherman, and he called his boat the Stag's Head after Brading's famous lager beer. He painted The cottage a bright white with red trim. Described as a "hail fellow well-met." Dave Ault was a friend to everybody on the beach.

When he came down on the weekends, he'd bring down a few cases of beer along with glasses and ashtrays. Dave supplied many of the prizes for the Civic Holiday weekend get-together. He was also involved in running the games, and he was a real community-oriented type of guy. Dave was an Englishman and his brewery, Brading was small compared to their big competitors of Molson and Labatts.

In 1954 Mr. Ault sold the cottage to Mrs. Winifred Murphy Pugsley. The cottage soon fell into disrepair and was abandoned for many years until 1962 when it was torn down. Davelie was the only cottage on the beach that had canvas awnings and those awnings were considered quite the thing for West Beach at the time. Dave's son David Jr. married Dorothy Ann Currie, who was the local beach lifeguard. Dave's oldest daughter, Shirley married Chuck Ormsby from Cove Road. Over the years many summer beach romances turned into long-time relationships and marriages.

Auntie Robinson at Davelie Cottage

Leaside

One of only two cottages (the other being Moonshine) that were like the television show Cheers, "where everyone knows your name." Leaside belonged to the Richard Hughes family for many years. Richard was related to the famous Sir Sam Hughes, Canada's Minister of the Military during WWI. Built-in 1905 Leaside is one of the oldest cottages on the beach. Leaside's origins are shrouded in mystery, the fact that it stood on Liberty Street South across the road from the present-day Flying Dutchman Hotel is beyond dispute. The mystery lies in how it got from there to the beach. An old story on the beach was that it was Mrs. Hughes mother's house and that the family, after her death dragged the house down to the beach on the ice during the winter of 1905. Around 2003 Colonel Alton Hughes came to visit Gary Cole and solved the mystery. He told Gary that his father had torn down the house and used the lumber to rebuild it on West Beach. When it was first put up, it had a clear view of the beach from its L-shaped veranda. Soon surrounded by many new cottages, all the Hughes could see was everyone else's back door.

Is it haunted? West Beach legend has it that Richard's mother died in her rocking chair in the living room. Having spent many nights in Leaside cottage, Gary Cole states that he never experienced anything remotely paranormal. Although the thought was always there in the back of his mind: "is this cottage haunted?" Sometimes the rocking chair would mysteriously start to rock back and forth for no apparent reason.

In 1962 Vera Bains (Richard's daughter) sold the cottage to Gary Cole, and he made several renovations to it. The cottage had two bedrooms upstairs and the veranda was turned into a kitchen and a bedroom. Altered, so it faced the lake rather than the marsh the cottage was rented out for many years. First to a family named Flanagan, and then to Steve Rider, and then to the Hipwell family (from Toronto) and lastly, to Gail and Chuck MacDonald. In 1996 Leaside was sold to Mike Lootsma, who also made many improvements.

Unfortunately, Leaside cottage no longer exists.

Brooks Cottage – Boarding House #3

Next to nothing is known about the Brooks family after who this cottage is named. At one time, the cottage was part of the Boarding House complex, and Mr. Berry and the late Charlie Servers rented it during the summer to various people such as Forest Dilling. For some time, there was an L-shaped veranda on the main floor while upstairs, there were two bedrooms. Eventually, Charlie Severs modified the L-shaped veranda so that it faced the lake.

In approximately 1954, Charlie Severs sold the cottage to Mrs. Winifred Murphy Pugsley, who winterized it and lived there year- round with her daughter Pat and her grandchildren. Mrs. Pugsley's son Grant (who owned a Ford Edsel) liked to dress in a Zoot Suit which was in fashion back in the mid-1950s. Mrs. Pugsley's grandchildren's names were: Ricky, Tommy and Linda Conahan. At one time, Mrs. Pugsley owned a hot dog stand business on Wasaga Beach.

The cottage sat abandoned for many years, and the Town of Newcastle eventually expropriated it and four others. They had the cottage torn down (with the assistance of a few neighbours) in 1979.

Seldom Inn

Built by brothers Frank and Norm Bottrell, and their sisters, this small cottage started as a little more than a one-room cabin which was painted yellow with red trim. It was enlarged over the years and used exclusively in later years by Norm, his wife Helen, and sons Jim, John and Harvey. Harvey, who was six months older than Gary Cole was a soprano singer, who sang in the Saint Mike's choir. He would always sing "Danny Boy" during the Civic holiday long weekend get-togethers on the beach. Harvey went to work for American Motors and eventually worked for the Chrysler Corporation. Johnny Bottrell was a school teacher, and the oldest, brother Jimmy worked for I.B.M. in Chicago. The Bottrell brothers, Norm and Frank we're like the characters Mutt and Jeff. Frank was quite short and a little bit on the plump side while Norm had a tall bean pole type of body shape. Both Norm and Frank worked in the Goodyear plant in Bowmanville. But around the time of the First World War Norm moved to the New Toronto Goodyear plant while Frankie stayed at the Bowmanville plant where he became a supervisor. In the beginning, the brothers pitched a tent on West Beach but once during a big storm their tent was blown away. So the two boys decided just to put up a shack instead of a tent, but their two sisters said: "who wants to live in a shack"? So it was decided that they'd build a proper cottage, and they all took shares in it. Frank, who never had any children was quite an outgoing person, while Norm was rather straight-laced. Frank was a big pigeon fancier, he used to show pigeons at the C.N.E. in Toronto, and he also enjoyed pigeon racing enthusiast. Frank had an 18-foot slate blue canoe which he called the: "U.N.I." It had cushions, and Frank enjoyed taking ladies from the beach for rides on the lake. Frank never owned a car, and he always rode a bicycle. Even when he was off the bike, he would walk around the beach with his pant clips on his pant leg. Frank lived in Carlyle Avenue where the Goodyear houses still are today. Norm lived in Toronto with his three sons. Norm was most often at the cottage during the summer while Frank would open the cottage in the spring and close it in the fall and Frank did most of the cottage renovations. Frank built the cottage to his shorter height specifications, and it must have been trying for Norm to get around inside as he was constantly bumping his head.

In the late 1980s, Ben and Jean Severs bought Seldom Inn. Since the owners were seldom in it was thought to be well named. It is also one of the only two cottages which still had an outhouse.

Irmadell

Irmadell is a sizeable green cottage with white trim and constructed in a modified version of the West Beach style. Irmadell is almost a carbon copy of El Dorado and built by Charlie Heal for M.T. Fowler in 1915. It was occupied for many years by Mr. Alf Fowler, his wife Gertie and their family. The cottage was named after his daughter Irma "Toots" Fowler, later her married name was Redman. This cottage, unlike Seldom Inn, was never empty. There was the Fowler clan, (Ab, and Normie Lowe and son Bob), the Redmans, (Ralph, Irma, and their children Joan, Doug, and Ann), Mrs. Gertie Fowle's sisters Ruby Benneyworth and Irene Finlay and Irene's granddaughter Caroline along with many visitors. In fact on the West Beach Irmadell was a place where it was always happening. It is still painted green and white and occupied throughout the summer by Alf's daughter Miss Shirley Fowler. Mrs. Fowler's sister Ruby Bennyworth came from Nashville Tennessee, where she was a receptionist in the Andrew Jackson Hotel. She knew all the country stars right from Ernest Tubb to Hank Snow, right up to Elvis Presley. In Nashville, they referred to her as "Miss Benny," and when she came to visit the beach, she would always bring autographs for her nieces and nephews. Ruby came up every summer to spend a couple of weeks with her sister. She had two sons Walter and Abe, and they were both pilots in the American Air Force. After WWII, Abe was flying a spy plane (like Gary Francis Powers flew). Abe flew out of Turkey, where the US was spying on the Russians. It was here that Abe's plane was shot down and he lost his life as a result. Mrs. Finley lived in St Catharines, where her husband was a tinsmith; she would bring her granddaughter Caroline and spend the summers on the beach. On a typical weekend, there would have been 10 to 15 people in this cottage. Mrs. Finley did all the cooking on a wood stove with no help. No one else was allowed to go in the kitchen as that was her private domain. Irma Fowler's nickname was "Toots," and she lived in Toronto. Their children's names were Joanie (who was around Gary Cole's age) Doug and Anne, who was the youngest child. Toot's grandson, Timmy Knight, is just retired from the Durham Regional Police and he still comes and visits the cottage quite a bit. Abe Lowe was Mrs. Fowler's brother, and in that family, there were also three girls and Abe, who was the youngest child and the only boy. Abe married Norma McCormick and everyone on the beach called Norma's mother: "Mrs. Mac."

In later years Abe was the man around the house because he looked after things. Alf Fowler passed away at the young age of sixty. The Lowes only had one son, Bobby Lowe who is just about Gary Cole's age. Now Bobby has become the man of the house, and he looks after the cottage for his cousin Shirley. Bobby has done many renovations and improvements to the cottage, in recent years. He put all new shutters on the cottage and had it painted. Bobby also put in a shower, and last year he set a metal roof on the cottage. Shirley Fowler, who never married is now the longest resident on the beach in terms of age. She has been on the beach since her birth, and she was 97 years of age (in 2019). There used to be a lot of parties at Irmadell with numerous neighbours invited to join in. They would have a few hors d'oeuvres and sing a few songs; Irmadell was a real family place.

Veletta

Situated behind Bert Edward's lot, this cottage initially belonged to Miss Cameron and was called Sunnyside. In the 1930s, Miss Cameron's nephew, Bert Latimer, tore down Sunnyside and built Veletta, from the salvaged lumber. He named the new structure Veletta after his two vivacious daughters Velda and Zetta, who, along with their husbands and children, used the cottage until the 1970s. Bert Latimer was a laugh-a-minute kind of guy; Bert was the kind of guy that everybody liked. He was good with kids and never had a bad word to say about anybody. Bert served in WWI, and when he came back from the war, he was thrilled to land Dory Edwards, (the girl next door) as his wife. Dory's first husband had been tragically died of the flu after WWI.

Bert worked in Toronto at the Queen's Key liquor store, which is the number one liquor store in Ontario. Bert had two daughters; the oldest was Velda; she was a beautiful girl and a dead ringer for Joan Blondell. The younger sister Zetta was probably one of the most beautiful woman who ever to graced the sands of West Beach. Velda eventually married Bob McLeish of Toronto, and their two daughters were Carol Anne and Alexandria. Alexandria became a model and did many commercials, including Labatt Blue beer. Zetta married Len Rider also from Toronto, and their three children were: Steven, Sydney (named after Sid Smith) and Dougie. Len Rider was the President of the Beach Association for many years. Len was a dead ringer for President Kennedy. Besides his similar appearance, he also smoked cigars, and his hair was the same.

They were all good people who did a lot for the beach. They expanded Veletta at least twice by changing the two bedrooms into a kitchen and a living room and then adding four bedrooms on to the back of the building.

Sunnyside

Sunnyside was one of the oldest cottages on the beach, this small cottage was built by Herb Dilling (who was Forest Dilling's father) around 1900. It was little more than a shack with an open veranda. Miss Cameron (who was an aunt of Bert Latimer) bought the cottage during the First World War. Bert Latimer salvaged as much of the lumber out of it as he could and built his cottage, looking towards the Dancehall and called it: "Valletta."

Many years later, Tom Wright placed a converted boat house on the lot which he used as a cottage and called it: "The Sand Blows Inn". Tommy Wright later bought a cottage lot on Pigeon Lake north of Gannon Narrows, and he moved the boathouse there.

Sunnyside Cottage 1920 women dressed in drag

Sunnyside Cottage 1905

Tom Wright & Gary Cole at "The Sand Blows Inn" 1974

Welcome Inn - Granny's

Appropriately named Welcome Inn and built in the typical West Beach style, this cottage was built around WWI by carpenter Sam Henning for Mrs. Annie "Granny" Edwards. Her daughter, Dorry, (who married their next-door neighbour Bert Latimer), and her son Bert lived with her and her sailor son Alf. When Gary Cole was a boy, he and his friends would stand in wonderment when Bert would raise the Naval Ensign flag above the cottage, and later Alf would arrive, complete with captain's hat, for his annual weekend at the cottage. One of Gary's most memorable days occurred a few years later when Alf presented the Naval Ensign flag to him. Gary still has the flag (tattered as it is), and Gary had the pleasure of raising it at the West Beach reunion in 1998. Mrs. Edwards was a short woman who only stood around five foot, but she was quite wiry and without an ounce of fat on her. One day when she was sweeping down the inside of her cottage, Gary Cole and his mother heard a tremendous crash. When they ran over to Edward's cottage, they found Granny lying on the floor. She had fallen off the living room table where she had been standing to reach the cobwebs. The Edwards were British immigrants from England, and both of the Edwards' sons fought in the 1st World War. Bert, who never married was gassed at the Second Battle of Ypres, where the German Army used mustard gas for the first time. Being gassed affected Bert's health for the rest of his life, and as a result, he was never able to work. He would spend every summer at the cottage with his mother. Bert had an English girlfriend named Edith Greenstreet, and Edith's occupation was making paper flowers. She kindly taught this art to many of the girls who lived on the beach. Bert, unfortunately, died in the mid- 1950s from complications due to the gas that he inhaled while he was in the war. The other brother Alf (who didn't come to the cottage that often) also served in the 1st World War. He had gone back to England and enlisted in the Royal Navy. Alf fought at the Battle of Jutland in 1916, and he was in London, during one of the Zeppelin raids.

After the war, Alf lived in Toronto on Beaconsfield Court, and he was in the Naval Reserve on the HMCS York in Toronto harbour. It was there that he achieved the rank of chief petty officer (the equivalent to a sergeant major in the army). Alfie also served in World War II. Alf's son Frankie also served in the Canadian Navy, and he was one of the two youngest sailors on a Canadian ship when it landed at New York City. There is a picture of them with Gracie Fields when she came to tour the vessel and entertain the sailors. Alf also helped the Canadian armed services with recruitment during the Korean War in 1952 and 1953. As a result of this, Alf could truthfully say he saw naval service in all three wars. Alf was always immaculately dressed on the beach, where Alf liked to wear his Petty Officer's cap and white duck pants. Alf also liked to decorate his cottage with naval signal flags as he was "all navy all the time."

After Granny Edwards passed away, Gary Cole bought the cottage. It was traditionally painted cream with brown trim, but Gary changed the colour scheme to lime green with orange trim. The cottage later belonged to Gary's cousins: Rolly and Brenda Lloyd (who were part of the Henning family).

Winiverfuss

Winiverfuss (which represented "We Never Fuss") was erected in the 1920s and sported a cottage style roof. Built by Bill Street of Toronto and occupied by his family for many years. One of Gary Cole's earliest memories was playing with Bill's grandson Dave Parker. Mr. Street was a school janitor from Toronto, and he had a rather large family. His oldest daughter Jean who was born with a disability, liked to sit on the cottage veranda and chat with the passers-by as they walked up to the Dancehall. His other daughter Winifred married Jack Cully, who she had met on the beach. His next daughter Madeleine married Jack Parker, who she had also met on the beach. Their youngest daughter's name was Peggy, and she married Ross Wright. So on any given weekend, with all their children, spouses and grandchildren gathered together, so their cottage was always full. Gary Cole's friend, David Parker, was one of their favourite grandchildren.

Mrs. Ruby Street and her husband Bill lived in Toronto near Danforth Avenue, as did the Millins and the Fowlers. These three families formed a clique on the beach. Mr. and Mrs. Street would take their daughter Jean to the movies at least once a week, where she would sit in the aisle in her wheelchair. When Gary was a boy, Mrs. Street (who loved children) would tell him and his friends the plots of many of the movies that she had seen. Most of these were cowboy movies with stars such as Randolph Scott.

The cottage was next sold to Bill Sever's Sr. (Gary Cole's grandfather), who named it "Pop's Place." He only owned it for a few years, and then he sold it to Milt Corson and his wife Marg, who named it "Mom's Place" and they painted it a vivid pink. They lived in the cottage year-round for many years with their large family. Their children's names were: Linda (the oldest), Christine, Darlene, Deborah and their adopted son, Donnie. Marg's mother, Mrs. Summerscales, lived there with them as well, and that's when the cottage was renamed "Mom's Place." Mrs. Summerscales, while small in stature, was a real go-getter; she was very active in the local Legion, and she loved to go to bingo every week. It was almost like a family reunion when they all got together on the beach. There would be five families gathered, and they would have pot-luck, lounge on the beach, play horseshoes and penny- ante poker.

Bill & Ruby Street with Dave Parker & Dancehall Behind

Tacoma - Fernleigh

Sporting a cottage style roof, Tacoma owners were Mrs. Flossy Matthews, her son Andy, daughter Betty (Mrs. Lionel Parker) and their families. In 1972 Tacoma was used by Betty's son Doug during his honeymoon.

Gary Cole recalls asking Mrs. Matthews about the name "Tacoma," and she said that was its name when they bought the cottage and so they simply left it the same. Thus the origin of this cottage name is also unknown. In the First Nations language, the word Tacoma means a meeting place, so perhaps this is the origin of its name. Mr. Matthews was born in Cork Ireland and fought in the First World War. Mrs. Matthews' given name was Florence, and she was a lovely lady. Her son Andy worked for the CNR Railway out of Montreal. They had a daughter Betty who married Lionel Parker. Lionel was a plumber in Bowmanville.

Charlie Severs bought the cottage and enlarged it and wrecked it, (according to Doug). Ben and Jean Servers, who now own the cottage, renamed it Fernleigh. Fernleigh is a common word used for various locations around Australia, and has its basis in the vegetation of the area. 'Fern' - after the plant and 'Leigh' - (derived from Old English leah) meaning a meadow or forest clearing. Although presently clad in aluminum siding, the cottage still retains its traditional cream and brown colour. The exact age of the cottage is unknown, although it is believed that its origins date to the 1930s.

The Matthews eventually sold the cottage to Charlie Severs, who remodelled and enlarged it to almost twice its original size. After Charlie passed away, his son Bill Severs took over Tacoma and lived in it year-round. Bill made many improvements inside, including installing insulation and electric heat. Eventually, Bill went out to British Columbia, where he worked as an electrician on construction. Bill also worked in the Queen Charlotte Islands and the Bay Area of San Francisco. During this time, Irene Severs (Charlie's wife) gave the cottage to Gary's cousin Marnie Eccles who, in turn, gave it to her parents Ben and Jean Severs. Ben served in the Canadian military, and while stationed in St John's Newfoundland, he met his future wife, Jean. They married before Ben went overseas, so Jean came up to Ajax, Ontario, where she still lives. Jean is 92 years old now and still lives in Ajax.

Boskey Dell

Boskey Dell had initially been a garage located somewhere in the town of Bowmanville. It was moved down to the West Beach in the 1920s and additions to the front and back were made by Bruce Lunney. It was painted green with white trim, and initially, shingles covered the exterior walls.

It was bought in about 1939 by Mrs. Jack Cole (Gary's grandmother) and Miss Marg Cole (Gary's aunt), and occupied by Gary's parents, Fred and Edith Cole. In June of 1942 at nine months of age, Gary took his first steps on Boskey Dell's verandah. It was later owned for several years by Walter Cole, Gary's uncle who renamed it Waltz Inn. The cottage originally had a small living room, a small kitchen and two small bedrooms. When Walter bought the cabin, he took one of the bedrooms out to make the living room larger. Walter's son Merle slept in the back bedroom while Walter and his wife slept on pull-out cots in the living room. Walter came from Bowmanville, and his wife came from Courtice, and he worked as a barber in Oshawa.

Other Boskey Dell owners were Dave Ford and Brian Fox-Male, who were commonly known as "the boys." During the time of their ownership (5-7 years) the cottage was called "Foxy's Lair" and was the site of many beach parties. Brian Fox-Male came from a prominent English family, and his father was a colonel in the British Army back when India was still part of the British Empire. The Colonel commanded a regiment of the King's Own Royal Gurkha Rifles. Brian attended the Wellesley Military Academy, which was a prominent British boarding school which was run along military lines. The school was named after Arthur Wellesley the Duke of Wellington. Brian was also a Rhodes Scholar, and when the war started, he joined the army as a private. His regiment was stationed in Sussex (or perhaps Surrey). Brian spent 1939-40 stationed on an island in the Thames River. Later he transferred to the intelligence corps where he served in the Greek theatre. Brian's family came from Cornwall in the far southwest of England, and at that time, his family's name was "Male." Back in the 1700s, the Male family were known as "wreckers." They would rearrange the lighthouse lights so that ships would deliberately crash onto the rocks at night. The wreckers would then salvage the cargo and kill any members of the crew that survived the crash so there would be no witnesses. The legend of the family was that one of these crew members put a curse on the Male family before being killed. The curse stated that the firstborn of each subsequent Male family generation would die before he came into his inheritance. The curse held for 2-3 generations until Brian's great, great, great, great, grandmother decided to hyphenate the family's name with her maiden name of "Fox" to break the curse.

David Ford (who worked in the men's department of Robert Simpson's main store in Toronto) came from the town of Portneuf Quebec. David's father was a vital Industrialist in Portneuf, where he owned a paper mill. David's cousin was Glenn Ford, the famous Hollywood movie actor, who was also born in Portneuf. He appeared with Rita Hayworth in the great movie Gilda.

The next owners were an English fellow named Dave Dobson and his French Canadian wife, Sunny. They occupied the cottage for approximately two years, during which time they lived in it all year round. Dave Dobson saw service during WWII at the Battle of the River Plate (the first naval battle of WWII) during which the German battleship Graf Spee was sunk. The Dobsons eventually abandoned the cottage, and in 1992 it was demolished.

Belhaven

For many years this cottage belonged to the Hutton family, and they had a daughter named Marg who became a great swimmer. She did her swim training at the West Beach back in the 1930s along with Ernest Vervcotter, the legendary "Black Shark" of Germany. Marg Hutton excelled in synchronized swimming as well as long-distance swimming. Back in the 1920s and 1930s, the popularity of swimming and the swimmers were prevalent. Some examples are George Young from Toronto who swam the Straits of Juan de Fuca and Florence Chadwick who swam the English Channel along with the German: "Black Shark." There were also endurance races at the CNE where swimmers (including Vercotter) would swim 15 miles and more back and forth in front of the CNE. At one time Newcastle Beach resident Ernest Vervcotter came to West Beach where he met Marg Hutton. Their friendship included swimming and training together in front of the West Beach cottages.

Belhaven had three bedrooms, a large kitchen and a veranda. One summer the Hutton's rented the cabin for a couple of weeks. One day there was a knock on Cole's cottage door. The woman who had rented the Hutton cottage asked Gary's mom if she could "borrow a knife and a fork and a spoon?" This request to borrow things repeated itself two or three more times over the next few days. Eventually, Gary's mom asked the woman, "why are you coming here asking to borrow things?" The woman said that: the Hutton's had left them a note saying: "if there's anything that you need just go next door and ask."

One summer the Hutton family decided to rent out Belhaven, and in the renting family, there was a young fellow who got the nickname: "Henry Aldridge" from the radio show of the same name. Henry started delivering the Toronto Telegram newspaper on the beach. Delivering the Telegram was in direct competitor of the Toronto Star. The Star was already being offered by the Dilling boys who had established many customers on the beach. One day the Dilling boys set up a booby trap to spook the Henry Aldridge boy and sabotage his newspapers. They dropped a large tree branch across the road in front of Henry's bicycle and scattered his newspapers all along the back road. Back in the late 1930s early 1940s, there was an intense newspaper competition between the Toronto Star and the Telegram. At one time the Telegram dropped the price of their newspaper by three cents, and this caused many people to stop getting the Star which cost five cents. This price drop caused many hard feelings in the Dilling family.

Elwood Ellis of Toronto later owned the cottage. Elwood painted it white with royal blue trim, and he called it: "Belhaven" after the Toronto street where he lived. Mr. Ellis, his wife Marjorie and son Doug were one of the most unusual families ever to inhabit Bowmanville Beach. When Mr. Ellis took over the Belhaven cottage, he updated it extensively. Elwood put in interior walls, a fireplace and cement steps. He was an engraver by trade, and he had many magnifying lenses which he used to engrave small items. Elwood also engraved Black Cat cigarette boxes, and Elwood gave one to every child on the beach. Each box has a wood and metal plaque on which he had nailed a carpet tack, and on the carpet tack, he had engraved The Lord's Prayer. A magnifying glass was needed to read it as it was so small. Mr. Ellis was quite eccentric and a loner who didn't fit in with the rest of the beach population. Mrs. Ellis, while a little bit more outgoing than her husband, was also somewhat reclusive. Mr. Ellis' son had a cedar-strip canoe and a motorboat, and he loved to fish.

Belhaven cottage no longer exists on the beach.

Palais Royal

This large and somewhat dilapidated two-story cottage was built in 1910 for Bowmanville shopkeeper Mrs. Mary Ann "Nana" Keys, mainly out of packing crates. The brand name of: "Robinson's Jams" could be seen stamped on the cottage walls. It was originally a two-story cottage with the front of the second story veranda (which had a metal railing) open to the elements. The first floor also had a porch, and inside there was a large kitchen. Orange crates were used as kitchen cupboards and nailed to the wall. The occupants of the cottage had to sleep in a second-floor loft which was only accessible by a ladder as there was no stairway.

It was later owned by Royal Quinn, who painted the cottage a shocking purple colour and named it Palais Royal. After World War II it was rebuilt by his father "Pop" Quinn as a one-story cottage with a West Beach cottage style roof. Royal Quinn and his wife had three children whose names were: Joan, Ann and Leona.

Royale sold the cottage to the Charles Butler family who lived in it year-round for many years. Charles and his wife Jean lived there with his father (also named Charles), his mother, and his two stepsons. Jean also had a son and a daughter, and after Charles passed away, Jean moved away from the cottage and found an apartment in downtown Bowmanville.

All the kids on the beach were afraid of Palais Royal because of its spooky appearance. There was a 10-foot by 10-foot building in the backyard which the icemen used to store their ice. Unfortunately, this cottage was demolished many years ago and no longer exists on the beach.

X.T.C.

From the mid-1930s to the 1940s, this cozy cottage was owned and occupied by Ed and Elsie Luttrell and their daughter Doris. Ed Luttrell's father had owned a bakery in Bowmanville in the early 1900s. Ed later moved to Toronto, where he landed an excellent job with the stock brokerage firm of Dunn and Bradshaw. Ed was also the President of the West Beach Beach Association for many years. Ed Luttrell had a model of a sailboat that Gary Cole had admired for many years, and when Gary was around ten years old, and the Luttrells were moving away, Mr. Luttrell gifted the boat to Gary (which he still has it to this day). Ed sold the cottage to the Dorney family, and he bought another cottage further up the road at Crystal Beach.

The new owner, Art Dorney (a former Toronto fireman), bought the cottage for his mother, Mrs. Dorney and her sister Mrs. Mushing. They shared the cottage along with his niece and nephew: Carol and Fred Dorney. Art had served time in the Canadian Army and found himself stationed in Halifax during the time of the Great Riot, which took place there in May 1945. Art's nephew, Fred Dorney, had been like a big brother to Gary Cole when they were kids together on the beach. At that time, there were boxing competitions sponsored by the Toronto Fire Department. Fred Dorney competed in these and did very well when he was 15 or 16 years old.

After time passed, XTC cottage fell into disrepair and sadly, the cottage exists no longer.

The Ross Cottage

In the 1940s this small cottage with a West Beach cottage style roof, belonged to well known and respected Bowmanville theatre owner Tommy Ross. Tommy was very active on the West Beach in those days and instituted the idea of building the "Tommy Ross Road" through the marsh, which bypassed Mrs. Winifred Fox's hated Fox Gate.

Tommy Ross was a very community-oriented person and a strong promoter and advocate of Bowmanville back in-the-days when it was still a one-horse town. Tommy sponsored the Bowmanville hardball baseball team, which he called the Royals after his theatre, and the team played on a field behind Bowmanville's first high school on Queen Street (which has recently been demolished). At one time, when Tommy donated a large Union Jack flag to the St John's Church in Bowmanville, some of the parishioners objected and didn't want to accept the flag, because Tommy owned the theatre in Bowmanville. The minister of St. John's Church, Reverend Canon Spencer had an affection and respect for Tommy. Reverend Spencer had the flag put up above the door at the back of the church, where it stayed for many years. He said to Tommy: "if you take one end of the flag. I'll take the other, and we'll put it up together." During the war, Mr. Ross would organize different drives to help with the war effort, and he had children collect tin cans to be melted to make steel. If the children collected a certain amount of cans, they were allowed free admission to the matinee at his movie theatre. Tommy also had children collect milkweed plants for their sap, which at the time was believed to be an important source latex sap for the war effort, and the white fluff from the milkweed plant was also thought to be useful as a stuffing for life preservers. In 1944 Tommy Ross had a contest where the child who collected the most milkweed plants would win a prize. The Dillings (Gary Cole's neighbours on the beach) had collected a lot of milkweeds, and on the day it was to be delivered, Gary's father Fred, took the rumble seat out of his car and put a wooden box in the back, so it became a kind of small pickup truck. The milkweed was put in the box and taken to the Tommy Ross collection area for storage. The children collected so much milkweed, two or three trips were required. Wallace Dilling won the prize for most milkweed collected, and he won the prize of a catcher's mitt. Tommy Ross life had a sombre and tragic ending when he fell asleep in his Lazy Boy chair while smoking a cigar at his home in town, and the smoke contributed to his death. When Tommy Ross lived in the cottage, the members of his family were: his sons Tommy Jr., and Danny, and his daughter Geraldine. The Ross boys built a boat named the "Skyler," which was about 10 feet long and built as a paddle-wheeler, which the boys used to paddle up and down the river.

After the Ross family left the beach, a fellow named Marv Allin and his wife Marg bought the cottage, where he lived year-round for two or three years. Mr. Allin had three daughters, one of whom was named Judy.

Later "Leaping Lew" Burton (who was a laugh a minute kinda guy) bought the cottage. Leaping Lew tried unsuccessfully once to write a book of poetry, he was reasonably good at rhyming but not very good on rhythm; Gary Cole still has a copy of his book. Lew was very community-minded on West Beach, where he helped repair the wooden boardwalks.

Later owners were: Joe Kilpatrick and his wife Pearl (for two or three years) and their children: Ricky, Joey, and Diane. Unfortunately, the Ross cottage is now only a melancholy memory as it was torn down in 1972.

Linger Longer - For Rest

This board and batten cottage initially was white with red trim. It had a gable roof with the gable facing to the front, and this was differed from most of the other beach cottages. Linger Longer was built by Herb Dilling after he left his previous cottage (Sunnyside). Herb Dilling lived on Ontario St. in Bowmanville. He was a house painter by trade.

Around 1940 Forest Dilling bought his father's cottage for $500.00. Forest and Lillian Dilling and their children: Wally, Gary and Catherine moved in around that time. Forest improved the cottage putting on insul-brick siding, removing the fireplace and changing the cottage's name to: "For Rest." Around 1947-48, Forest winterized the cottage, and the family lived into it year-round, making them one of the first families to live on Bowmanville Beach throughout the winter. Forest was very involved with the Bowmanville Museum right from its inception in 1961. He was also one of the first bird banders in Canada at that time. Starting in 1936, Forest was instrumental in studying the migration of birds between the US and Canada. Forest kept very detailed records of the birds that he banded with the help of Gary Cole. They worked together to catch the birds, band them and then release them. In the 1930s Forest applied to train as an RCAF pilot at the Oshawa Airport. When World War II broke out, Forest asked to join the RCAF, but he was turned down because of asthma and his age.

Forest was a leap-year baby being born on February 29, 1904. Forest was a local Bowmanville and West Beach historian, having spent practically his whole life on the beach. A great deal of Gary Cole's knowledge of Bowmanville Beach history he learned from Forest Dilling. Forrest's wife, Lillian, was a knowledgeable leathercraft instructor who was proficient in creating fascinating articles out of leather. After WWII she also worked for the federal government's Bureau of Statistics; going door-to-door and asking people questions about their homes and their contents. With the rationing during WWII, this information was essential to the Canadian government. Although in today's world of privacy concerns, people would hesitate to supply such personal information. The two Dilling sons Wally and Gary were like big brothers to Gary Cole, and he helped them with their Toronto Star paper-route on the beach. Over time the Dilling's daughter Catherine took over the paper route. Being good boaters and sailors, at one time or another, all three of the Dilling children had rowboats. They used their boats as a personal, unofficial ferry service, moving things and people across the river from East Beach to West Beach. For five cents, they would row people back and forth, mostly at night. Forest was also an accomplished kite builder and flyer. At one time Forest built a six-foot by four-foot kite. With its heavy string and crank, anchoring to the beach was necessary, to avoid lift-off. The Dilling boys at one time had three pet crows which they named Tom, Dick and Harry. One of the crows named Tom was notorious for stealing clothesline pegs and storing them in a hole in one of the willow trees. The Dilling boys had a huge tree fort in the back of their cottage. At one time one of Gary Cole's friends Teddy Hallman went missing although luckily he was later found sleeping in the tree fort. Because Teddy was so small, no one could figure out how he got up there.

Coal Hole

This cottage originally belonged to Bruce Murchison's father who came from Scotland and worked at a bank in Toronto. Around the beach, Bruce was quite well known. The Murchisons had a Scottish uniform with a kilt and all the trimmings. For three generations all of the family was photographed in that uniform. Bruce married Marian White who was Auntie Robinson's niece. Coal Hole had an L-shaped veranda (where the whole family slept) which surrounded a small kitchen/dining room area.

In the late 1920s to the Crookshank family of Toronto bought the cottage. They were also of Scottish descent, and it was during their ownership that the cottage was crushed by a fallen willow tree. The Crookshanks had a connection to the Van Dusen family who stored their boat in a boathouse on East Beach. The Crookshanks would drive to East Beach; get their boat and row to their cottage on West Beach. After being crushed by the fallen willow tree in 1934, it was rebuilt using the existing lumber, and a cottage-style roof was added. The stump of the enormous willow which fell across and crushed the original cottage was still there when Gary was a child. It was approximately 75 years old and 30 feet high. Another willow tree grew out of the original trunk, and this new willow grew to become three feet across at the trunk. Years later, after Coal Hole had been torn down, this tree also fell during a storm, and it landed precisely where the original Coal Hole cottage once stood. The original willow tree is still growing today even though it is now laying on its side on the ground.

Coal Hole was bought by Fred Cole, (Gary Cole's father) who painted it bright yellow with green trim. It also owned by Edie Cole's niece, Marion Henning. After the death of his mother, Gary gave the cottage to the Henning family, and it was also held for a brief time by Mike Lootsma.

When Gary's mom and dad lived in the cottage, it had a veranda and two bedrooms. Gary's dad glassed in the veranda and took the partition out, and this made an L-shaped living room/dining room, at the far end of which was a huge dining room table. Every year Gary and his family would arrive on the 24th of May weekend and stay until Thanksgiving. In later years Gary's father lost interest in Coal Hole cottage. Although his mother still loved it and it was her little bit of heaven.

Rendezvous

This two-story cottage was built in 1920 by Mrs. Susie Dunn of Toronto. Subsequent owners of the cottage were: Jack and Win Cullie, Tom Wright, Ron Parker, the Carpenters and the Henning family.

It was a ramble shack cottage until Jack and Win Cullie bought it. Jack fixed and cleaned it up quite a bit. When the Carpenters owned the cottage they rented it out quite often, and the renters would commonly be quite noisy. When the Cullies held it, Mrs. Cullie's mother, Mrs. Street, came and lived there and stayed all summer.

One of the few real tragedies on West Beach occurred there in 1940, with the tragic drowning death of a 9-year-old girl named Noreen. She was the daughter of a famous Toronto radio personality, and she was staying with Mrs. Carpenter's sister-in- law, at the time. Noreen had just arrived to spend a few weeks at the beach, and she had become very close friends with the Lawson family's daughter, who lived in the Dunn cottage, which was just opposite Rendezvous. One day the two girls were swimming in the river when the Lawson girl got in trouble, and one of the local beach men rescued her and brought her onto the shore. After reviving her, she revealed that Noreen had also been swimming in the river. Several rescuers searched for Noreen but to no avail. Mr. Dilling from the Dancehall arrived with his rowboat and a grappling hook. He searched up and down the river dragging the grappling hook behind his boat. Eventually, Noreen was finally located and brought onto the shore. While the rescuers attempted to revive Noreen, Dr. Rundle was sent for and asked to attend to an emergency on the beach. After his arrival, Dr. Rundle performed artificial respiration on her. While he was doing so, he asked two bystanders (Gary Cole's mother and Mrs. Currie) to rub the girl's legs in an attempt to increase her blood circulation. Eventually, Dr. Rundle sadly stated: "she's gone it's all over." Afterwards, Gary's mother and Mrs. Currie went to Cole's cottage to have coffee and calm their nerves. While there, they discussed the tragedy and they both agreed that while they were rubbing Noreen's legs, they could both feel her slip away. As a result of experiencing this tragedy, Gary's parents and the Currie's became best of friends. So traumatized was Mrs. Carpenter (who had brought Noreen to the Rendezvous cottage that day) that she packed up all of her belongings and left the beach, never to return. Even though Gary Cole was only four years old when this tragedy happened, he still recalls the events with a great deal of emotion, like it was yesterday. As tragic as it was, it was the only child drowning in the West Beach community over all the years it has been there.

The cottage known as Rendezvous was sadly torn down in 1993.

Rusty Nook

Mrs. Susie Dunn built this cottage around 1930, but unfortunately, its location was in the marsh. Suzie earned an income of sorts by baking pies, cakes and other baked goods and selling them out of her cottage. Mrs. Dunn would bake pies and cakes on a wood stove in her kitchen and sell them to the other beach residents.

Her grandson, Gordie Lawson built a 12 x 12 cabin beside Rusty Nook containing a bed, a couple of chairs and a table, making it the only cottage on the beach to be owned by a kid. There were always four or five boys hanging around Gordie's cabin, and these guys were like big brothers and treated Gary Cole with kindness. Their names were: Patty Doyle, Freddy Dorney, Roy and Ron Gorum and the Dilling boys. These friends spent a lot of time on Gordie's rowboat as well as shooting their BB guns which they often allowed Gary to take a turn shooting as well.

Suzie Dunn had initially built the cottage named Rendezvous, and in later years she moved across the road and built Rusty Nook. Suzie had three children: Stanley (who fought in WWI and he had also had been a fireman in the city of Toronto. In those days the fire trucks were very long with the ladders attached to them. Stanley's job was to sit at the very back of the fire truck where he operated a steering wheel. This steering wheel manoeuvred the end of the fire truck around corners. Suzie's second son Bill was a postman, and he also worked in the city of Toronto. Suzie had a daughter named Gladys who married a fellow named Lawson. Gladys would help Suzie bake and would even go around the beach and take orders from the other residents. Gladys would usually make her rounds just before the weekends so that the baked goods would be ready when the cottage husbands came back to the beach after working all week in the city of Toronto. Gladys had three children: Fay, Doris, and Gordie.

Mr. Billy Dunn was one of the guards at the railway crossing over which everyone had to cross to reach the beach. Mrs. Dunn lived at Rusty Nook for the last 4 or 5 years of her life, (she was disabled at the time and seldom ventured out of the cottage. There was a sitting room in Rusty Nook, and that is where Mrs. Dunn spent the majority of her time during her final years. She also stopped all of her baking of pies and cakes at that time.

Rusty Nook's outhouse location was at the end of a precarious walkway. Mrs. Dunn, because she wasn't walking too well in her later years, had trouble making the trip to it. A neighbour Mrs. Dilling was concerned about Mrs. Dunn's safety during her trip to the outhouse. Especially in the spring as Rusty Hook was quite often partially submerged underwater. Mrs. Dilling asked Gary Cole if he could cut out a section of Rusty Nook's wall and install a door in its place. That way, Mrs. Dunn could go directly to the outhouse without fear for her safety. Even though Gary was only 12 years old at the time, he completed the task, which was his first official carpentry job.

The Dunn family sold the cottage to Lornie Sills who was a bachelor, and he lived in Rusty Nook year-round. Tragically Lola Brown (a beach neighbour) found Mr. Sills dead in his cottage one day. Larry and Milley Saunders (who came from Newfoundland) were the next owners of Rusty Nook. They had four sons and two daughters, and after they moved away, Rusty Nook fell into disrepair, and was eventually torn down.

Lazy Days - Peggy's Cove

The last to be built on West Beach on an unnumbered lot, Lazy Daze stood in the area of the marsh. It was constructed by Ben Severs (Gary Cole's uncle and his mom's youngest brother) with the help of Bill Currie in 1949. At that the time it was tough to get lumber and Ben, who lived in Ajax got the lumber he needed from the demolition of the munitions buildings there, after the war. The cottage had red insul-brick siding, and a cottage-style roof, although the north side of the roof had a much steeper angle than the other three. The roof's unusual angle was because the lumber was not long enough and so splicing was necessary. Bill Currie designed the roof of this cottage even though he wasn't a real carpenter although he was good at that sort of thing. Bruce Lunny, who was a carpenter and lived up the road, looked at the cottage and said: "This will not stand up and will fall within two years." On this point, he was wrong as it stood for another 41 years until it was torn down in 1990.

Gary's other uncle, who owned the Dancehall asked Ben's wife, Jean to work at the Dancehall. Jean, who was supposed to be coming to the beach to have a relaxing holiday, found herself spending all her time working at the Dancehall instead. Eventually, Ben and Jean sold the cottage rather than have her quit her Dancehall job.

The next owners were Ed Hicks (a General Motors employee) and his wife who were originally from Nova Scotia. They lived in the cottage year-round along with their three children: Charles, Sheila and Margaret. Mr. Hicks, who was a carpenter by trade and he made many other improvements to the cottage, including adding insulation.

The next owners of the cottage were "Diamond Jim" and Peggy Sills. Jim was a huge man who unfortunately had a deformity in one of his arms. Mr. Sills tried to conceal his deformity as much as possible. Before his retirement and his move to the beach, Jim worked for a landscaping company in Courtice. They renamed the cottage Peggy's Cove in honour of Jim's wife, Peggy. At one time when the beach flooded and the cottage was sitting in water, Jim nailed a board to the front of the cottage which read: "Watergate." President Richard Nixon's downfall was happening at the time. Later because of a family dispute, Jim had to leave the cottage, and its ownership went to Peggy's children who did not use it nor keep it up.

Regrettably, Lazy Daze/Peggy's Cove was demolished in 1990 and no longer exists.

Uncle Tom's Cabin

This tiny cottage known as "Uncle Tom's Cabin," stood north of the ice houses and near Mrs. Dunn's cottage known as "Rusty Nook." The area where it stood later became the West Beach playground. Uncle Tom's Cabin builder, was well-known Bowmanville resident and entrepreneur, Tom Limer, who lived in a house on the corner of Ontario and Queen Streets.

The time period that this cottage existed on the beach is unknown, but Gary Cole speculates that it was not very long. And so over the years, it has entered the realm of mystery, and folklore, and people began to wonder if it ever even existed, or if it was just a figment of the older West Beach resident's imagination. Nonetheless, it did exist, and it has an exciting story to tell.

Over time as the water rose in the spring, it often became completely engulfed by the marsh. Gary Cole remembers, as a very young boy, seeing the outhouse for Uncle Tom's Cabin, standing forlorn and forgotten in the middle of the marsh; however, without a boat, there was no way access to it.

In 1942, Auntie "Winnie" Wanacott thought that perhaps she might buy Uncle Tom's Cabin. So one Sunday in the spring, Mrs. Wanacott and Fred Cole decided to take a canoe ride, from East Beach (even though Gary's dad could not swim) to inspect Uncle Tom's Cabin. They were able to paddle around it, and Gary's father advised Auntie Wanacott, "For God's sake, Winnie don't buy it." She later bought the Hodson cottage instead, which fortunately stood on higher, dry ground.

Uncle Tom's Cabin was subsequently dismantled and moved by Tom Limer, and incorporated into building part of a small house on Victoria or Albert Street in Bowmanville's South Ward.

In Conclusion

As I write the last pages of this book I thought long and hard on how to express my deep feelings for these few acres of constantly shifting sand. Then I remembered a few years ago my very good friend and Crystal Beach resident Susan Plumpton produced a picture book of the West Beach. As I re-read her closing remarks I realized I could do no better, here with Susie's kind permission are those words.

Reflections and Recollections

These photos capture the passing of many wonderful memories of gatherings and celebrations since these cottages were first built on West Beach from 1900 to 1912. Their historic beauty is evident in all the photos. The faces mirror the joy and comradery, the scenery mirrors the heart. We are at best mere guardians of the natural wonder of the shores of West Beach Lake Ontario. This beach is not part of our lives it is we who are privileged to be a part of it.

> "To see a world in a grain of sand and a heaven in a wildflower, to hold infinity in the palm of your hand and eternity in an hour."
>
> ~William Blake

Who but those who have had the rare gift of sharing these shores and these historic cottages could better understand Blake's eternal wisdom?